DIRECT MESSAGES

WORDS FROM
God's Prophets
TO *You*

DESERET
BOOK

All quotations come from Facebook or Instagram posts by the First Presidency and Quorum of the Twelve Apostles of The Church of Jesus Christ of Latter-day Saints between 2020 and 2025.

Compilation © 2025 Deseret Book Company

All rights reserved. No part of this book may be reproduced in any form or by any means without permission in writing from the publisher, Deseret Book Company, at permissions@deseretbook.com. This work is not an official publication of The Church of Jesus Christ of Latter-day Saints. The views expressed herein are the responsibility of the authors and do not necessarily represent the position of the Church or of Deseret Book Company.

This product offered by Deseret Book Company is neither made, provided, approved, nor endorsed by Intellectual Reserve, Inc., or The Church of Jesus Christ of Latter-day Saints. Any content or opinions expressed, implied, or included in or with this product are solely those of Deseret Book Company and not those of Intellectual Reserve, Inc., or The Church of Jesus Christ of Latter-day Saints.

DESERET BOOK is a registered trademark of Deseret Book Company.

Visit us at DeseretBook.com

Library of Congress Cataloging-in-Publication Data
CIP data on file
ISBN 978-1-63993-553-6

Printed in the United States of America
Publishers Printing, Salt Lake City, UT

10 9 8 7 6 5 4 3 2 1

DIRECT MESSAGES

CONTENTS

We Are All Sons and Daughters of God x

We Are Meant to Experience Joy 8

Jesus Christ Atoned for Us 14

God Has a Purpose for You 24

God Answers Our Prayers
and Gives Us Revelation 30

Heavenly Father Loves His Children 38

Foster Unity and Belonging 44

Study the Book of Mormon 50

Learn from Different Perspectives 60

Covenants Bring Power 64

Celebrate Christ's Resurrection 70

CONTENTS

Pursue Education and Lifelong Learning 82

Women Have Influence and Power 88

Family Is Essential 96

Disciples Follow Christ's Example. 104

We Can Repent and We Can Forgive 108

Give Thanks in All Things 118

Work Toward Worthy Goals. 126

Rely on the Holy Ghost 136

Trust in God 140

God Will Help Us Through Our Trials. 146

Be a Peacemaker. 154

The Lord Restored the Gospel
     Through Joseph Smith 160

Minister and Serve Like Christ 166

Teach the Gospel in the Savior's Way. 174

The Savior Promises Us Peace 184

Elevate Your Perspective 188

Priesthood Authority Blesses God's Children 194

Prepare for the Savior's Return 198

Taking the Sacrament Is a Privilege. 204

CONTENTS

Commandments Help Us Become Christlike. 208

Come to the House of the Lord 216

Jesus Christ Is the Strength of Youth 224

Feel the Joy of Christmas 230

Prophets and Apostles Testify
    of Christ and Speak Truth 238

DIRECT MESSAGES: Words from God's Prophets to You is an invitation—to pause, to listen, and to feel the voice of the Lord speaking to you through His chosen servants.

In a world that often feels noisy and uncertain, these messages from the First Presidency and Quorum of the Twelve Apostles of The Church of Jesus Christ of Latter-day Saints offer a steady, divine perspective. This collection draws from these leaders' recent social media posts—teachings meant to reach hearts in real time, in messages both formal and more conversational. They are brief but powerful expressions of living testimony for today.

The passages in this book are organized into central themes consistently emphasized by these inspired Brethren. You'll find calls to action that invite deeper discipleship, words of counsel that speak gently to life's challenges, eternal truths that bring clarity and peace, and heartfelt encouragement to keep going when things feel heavy.

With wisdom for every age and stage of life, these direct messages provide the reassurance that God is aware of you. Let these words from His prophets lift your heart and guide your steps. Whether you're seeking hope, answers, or a daily spiritual boost, this book reminds you that revelation is still flowing—straight to you.

WE ARE ALL *Sons* AND *Daughters* OF GOD

PRESIDENT HENRY B. EYRING

The Lord loves you. Whatever your circumstances, wherever you live, He loves you personally. He paid the price for all your sins. He has felt your pains and sorrows and so knows how to comfort you.

You are a beloved child of your Heavenly Father. You were nurtured by Him before you came into this world. He loves you and has blessed you every hour of your life. Many of those hours have been difficult, but Heavenly Father and Jesus Christ have never turned away from you. They have inspired Their servants to reach out to lift you up in your struggles. You have felt gratitude for that gift.

I know that Alma's counsel is true. He taught, "Counsel with the Lord in all thy doings, and he will direct thee for good; yea, when thou liest down at night lie down unto the Lord, that he may watch over you in your sleep; and when thou risest in the morning let thy heart be full of thanks unto God; and if ye do these things, ye shall be lifted up at the last day" (Alma 37:37).

ELDER PATRICK KEARON

My particular hope for you is that you will truly understand, much more deeply understand, that you are a daughter of God, that you are a son of God, and that that can be a new revelation, . . . or a renewal of an earlier understanding. . . . You're a cherished daughter; you are a precious son of God. And the powerful effect that has had on me since I discovered this truth in my mid-twenties—I can't really begin to describe, but it's profound. And I pray that you will understand this more deeply and more keenly.

ELDER NEIL L. ANDERSEN

The gospel of Jesus Christ gives us insight into who we truly are, why we are here on earth, how to continue along the covenant path, and where we can be for all eternity.

We are sons and daughters of God, here on earth to grow our faith in our Heavenly Father and His Son Jesus

We Are All Sons and Daughters of God

Christ, to learn by our experiences to follow Them and choose good over evil, striving to one day return to live with Them.

Knowing this, we are not afraid to be different. Jesus said of His disciples, "They are not of the world, even as I am not of the world" (John 17:16).

Let us look to the future with faith and hope. I promise that as you center your life in your faith in Jesus Christ and in the ordinances, covenants, and teachings of His holy house, you will see yourself for who you really are and who you can become.

PRESIDENT DALLIN H. OAKS

You know you are children of God, a uniquely divine heritage. God loves you. He is a powerful mentor, and He has promised to help you, if you but seek Him in the way He has taught. Establish in your mind and your personal priorities the powerful truth that you are a beloved child of God. His love endows you with the self-respect, the strength, and the motivation to move against whatever problems you face in your life and to never forget that his servants love you. We love you. In all our concerns as we work through all our challenges, we urge that we be of good cheer because

He has overcome the world. We can, too. Remember, our Father's plan is a plan of happiness.

PRESIDENT RUSSELL M. NELSON

During my earlier career as a heart surgeon, I stood in an operating room thousands of times. I even cared for wounded soldiers in MASH units during the Korean War. I have literally touched the hearts of men and women of many races and nationalities around the world. My prayers to God for His guiding help and the subsequent inspiration I received from Him were vital in every instance. In those operating rooms where life hung in the balance, I came to know that our Heavenly Father cares deeply for every one of His children. That's because we are His children. Differences in nationality, color, and culture do not change the fact that we are truly sons and daughters of God. And as a follower and witness of Jesus Christ, I have only come to understand that divine truth more deeply. Together, we proclaim the nobility of each precious son and daughter of God.

We are truly sons and daughters of God.

I have stated before and repeat today that racism, sexism,

We Are All Sons and Daughters of God

and a host of other -isms are universally and tragically limiting in the way we regard and treat each other. Any abuse or prejudice toward another because of race, nationality, gender, sexual orientation, culture, or any other identifiers is offensive to our Maker and defies the first and second great commandments: that we should love God with all our hearts and our neighbors as ourselves.

We firmly believe in the fatherhood of God and the brotherhood of man. We do not have to act alike or look alike to love each other. We can disagree on a matter without being disagreeable. If we have any hope of creating the goodwill and sense of humanity for which we all yearn, it must begin with each of us, one person and one interaction at a time. May we as sons and daughters of God, as eternal brothers and sisters, do all within our power to build up each other, learn from each other, and demonstrate respect for all of God's children. May we link arms in love and brotherhood.

ELDER RONALD A. RASBAND

Before speaking at a Primary devotional in Anchorage, Alaska, I asked some of my grandchildren what I should share with other children around their age.

"Pa, tell them that you know Jesus and that He loves them," they responded.

I took their suggestion to heart and made sure to promise each of those children that they are known by name by Heavenly Father, Jesus Christ, and the Holy Ghost. I also shared with them that God loves them.

The truths I shared with these precious children are the same truths I share with each of you.

Heavenly Father and Jesus Christ love us so much. We are God's children. We should share this important truth with everyone we know. We are never really alone. In Heavenly Father and Jesus Christ, we have constant friendship and support.

ELDER DIETER F. UCHTDORF

[In 2023] we joined with many commemorating Volkstrauertag, the German National Day of Remembrance, paying tribute to those who died in armed conflicts and victims of violent oppression because of their race, religion, or conviction.

In preparing for this year's ceremony, I considered if I was attending as a German, or as an American, or as a military representative, or as a Church representative. Although I am always all of those things, I decided to attend as a child of God.

We are all children of our Heavenly Father, regardless of our religion, our background, our upbringing, our race, our education, or our socioeconomic circumstances.

Let us remember what has happened in the past, learn from history, and become better friends, better neighbors, and better citizens. It is my hope that we may all find reconciliation and peace as we remember the past, live in the present, and prepare for a better future, always looking to Christ and remembering that we are fellow brothers and sisters.

> *Let us remember what has happened in the past.*

WE ARE *Meant* TO EXPERIENCE *Joy*

PRESIDENT RUSSELL M. NELSON

While we marvel at the accomplishments of men and women, all of that pales when compared with the creations and works of our loving Heavenly Father and His Beloved Son, Jesus Christ.

I both marvel and rejoice at the miracle of the birth of Jesus Christ, His life, His ministry, His mission, and more.

I marvel at the miracles required for the Prophet Joseph Smith to translate and publish the Book of Mormon, and I rejoice at the Restoration of The Church of Jesus Christ of Latter-day Saints.

I marvel at the faith of devoted Latter-day Saints around the world and rejoice that I have been blessed to meet countless individuals who have made my life so much richer.

I marvel at our Heavenly Father's plan of happiness and rejoice that families truly can be together forever.

DIRECT MESSAGES

May we strive ... to marvel and rejoice at the privileges and opportunities our Father in Heaven and our Redeemer Jesus Christ provide.

ELDER PATRICK KEARON

Long before I joined The Church of Jesus Christ of Latter-day Saints, I saw true joy in the lives of my friends who were members of the Church. Whenever I spent time with these friends, I simply felt joy radiate from them.

> *This is God's intent for our lives.*

At the time, I didn't understand why this struck me so significantly—but I certainly understand now. Our core belief is that we are meant to have joy. This is God's intent for our lives.

The Book of Mormon describes this belief perfectly for us:

"Adam fell that men might be; and men are, that they might have joy" (2 Nephi 2:25).

When I first read that verse, the joy I saw in the lives of my friends made absolute perfect sense to me.

To be clear, the joy described doesn't simply mean,

We Are Meant to Experience Joy

"Someday, maybe after this life is over, we'll have joy." While that is certainly true, it is also true that our Father in Heaven wants us to feel joy now.

The joy manifested in my friends' lives continues to inspire me today. I hope you will also recognize this truth and feel joy in your life today.

ELDER ULISSES SOARES

My dear friends, I rejoice in President Nelson's teachings that the joy we feel in our lives has little to do with the circumstances we face and everything to do with our focus on Jesus Christ. We know that redemption cometh in and through the Holy Messiah, who is the source of all joy. Having a clear understanding of that in our hearts, we can rejoice while having a bad day, a bad week, or even a bad year.

I testify that the Lord finds joy in us as we worship, love, and find joy in our labors in His vineyard. I witness that God's plan is to provide joy for us not only in this life but also throughout eternity.

DIRECT MESSAGES

ELDER PATRICK KEARON

Our Heavenly Father's plan is a plan of happiness. It's interesting, the names we give that same plan. We call it a plan of happiness, we call it a plan of mercy, we call it a plan of salvation, we call it a plan of redemption. These are different names we have to refer to our Father in Heaven's plan. We give it these names that are full of hope and full of joy and full of light. There's something in our mortal natures that accentuates our ability to see blockages and hindrances. But I am convinced that our Father in Heaven designed the plan to get you and me home. Each of us, with our sins, with our frailties, with our shortcomings, with our health that rises and falls, with our mental health that rises and falls, with our understanding that rises and we hope rises. It's all designed to get us home. This is the church of new beginnings. This is the church of fresh starts. This is the church of healing, of comfort. He's not putting up roadblocks in your way, you know. He's paving the path for you to get home safely to that beautiful, glorious place.

> *Our Heavenly Father's plan is a plan of happiness.*

We Are Meant to Experience Joy

PRESIDENT DALLIN H. OAKS

[My wife] Kristen and I love spending time together in the outdoors. We feel closer to God when we witness the beauty of the earth that He created.

The Book of Mormon teaches us: "All things denote there is a God; yea, even the earth, and all things that are upon the face of it, yea, and its motion, yea, and also all the planets which move in their regular form do witness that there is a Supreme Creator" (Alma 30:44).

How grateful I am for a loving Father in Heaven who has provided such a beautiful place for us to live, learn, and grow.

Jesus Christ Atoned for *Us*

PRESIDENT HENRY B. EYRING

Because Jesus Christ broke the bands of death, every one of Heavenly Father's children will rise again in a perfected, resurrected body that will never die. This sure promise can turn the sorrow of losing a loved one into hope, filling our hearts with peace and a joyful anticipation of reunion.

ELDER PATRICK KEARON

You are loved so much more than you can imagine. And to any of you who are thinking, *Not me*, I would say, particularly you. Particularly you. If any of you are feeling that you have made so many mistakes that you're not lovable, you're wrong. If you think that you've blown it in some terrible way and that you're now beyond the love of heaven or beyond anyone else, you are completely and utterly wrong. Yes, you've made mistakes. We all have. But He sent His Son to take your sins upon Him—and you're thinking, *My sins? Really?* Yes. Really. Wonderfully. Gloriously. Beautifully. Magnificently.

This glorious gift of repentance is... this beautiful opportunity to be relieved of our sins and mistakes. And if you're still thinking, *No, not me*, I want to say this to you: Don't think that you have done something that is beyond the infinite atoning gift of our beloved Jesus Christ.

ELDER QUENTIN L. COOK

The rain falls on the just and the unjust. And we know that in this life, it's a time for us to prepare to meet God. Just because we're living principles doesn't mean everything will go perfect in our lives or that we will be spared from the challenges that exist in life. What we do know is that the Savior's Atonement overcomes all of the things: overcomes death, overcomes sin for those who repent and receive covenants, and covers all those things that are unfair about life. The Savior and His Atonement are the answers to the most significant questions that we face.

> *The Savior's Atonement overcomes all things.*

Jesus Christ Atoned for Us

ELDER DALE G. RENLUND

A missionary asked me, "Are we hypocrites if we don't keep all the commandments that we teach to the people?" This is such a great question! I thought I would share my answer.... I know that I don't have to be perfect to be called to be a member of the Quorum of the Twelve Apostles. I know better than anybody that I'm not perfect. So do we have to be perfect to serve the Lord? Of course not. It isn't about that.

There's a big difference between rebellion and weakness. So it is hypocritical to teach a commandment that you don't intend to keep. That would be hypocritical. But to teach commandments and then stumble and repent—that's not hypocritical, because you are intending to keep the commandment. When we do things with real intent, it means that we intend to keep the commandments. So there isn't anything that's hypocritical about teaching about the covenant path or about teaching about God's commandments when you in fact intend to keep all of them. You know and can testify that keeping those commandments will bring blessings.

In the Book of Mormon, Moroni 6:8 says, "But as oft

as they repented and sought forgiveness, with real intent, they were forgiven." The hypocritical part comes if we make a mistake and don't repent and don't intend to repent. Integrity is when our actions and our beliefs are in complete harmony—it is how we try to live our lives. But is it hypocritical if we can't always do that? No, that's the whole point of repentance, isn't it? We can repent from those things that despite our good efforts we fail to do. Because of the Atonement of Jesus Christ, forgiveness is real.

PRESIDENT RUSSELL M. NELSON

If perhaps you feel you have strayed off the covenant path too far or too long, let me assure you that is not true. Through the Atonement of Jesus Christ your future can be bright, even brilliant. Come back to the joy and safety of the covenant path. We need you with us. Your ultimate success will come as you yoke yourself to Heavenly Father and Jesus Christ. I know that life with God is a life filled with peace, joy, and power. Resolve to live your life with God.

Jesus Christ Atoned for Us

ELDER DIETER F. UCHTDORF

The Christian world [remembers] Palm Sunday—that historic day when Jesus Christ, the King of kings, rode triumphantly yet humbly into the holy city of Jerusalem; it was a glorious and exciting moment.

But even more important was what Jesus did after He entered Jerusalem—even though much of it was done quietly, privately, even unnoticed by most people:

> *Life with God is a life filled with peace, joy, and power.*

- Jesus had a quiet Last Supper with His Apostles in the Upper Room.
- He walked into a garden called Gethsemane, and there—alone—He took upon Himself the sins of the world. He walked the winepress alone, and no one was with Him.
- Jesus hung on a cross, suffering a cruel and humiliating execution. He even felt forsaken by the Father.

As you intentionally make time and room in your life for quiet, small, simple but deeply spiritual moments—just as Jesus did—you will discover that the Lord knows you. He knows your heart. He knows your name.

DIRECT MESSAGES

These moments can be to you like that holy, peaceful moment on a beautiful spring morning outside an empty tomb, when a young woman was weeping and Jesus called her by name: "Mary."

Remember, the Savior knows your name too.

Just as He entered triumphantly into Jerusalem, the gentle Christ enters your life individually, if you will receive Him.

May our hearts be open as wide as the gates of Jerusalem to joyfully receive the Messiah, the Savior, the King of kings.

ELDER PATRICK KEARON

One of the great foundations of becoming a disciple is to have a really clear understanding in our heads and in our hearts of who our Father in Heaven is and who our Savior is and, particularly, how They feel about us. In 3 Nephi, the eleventh chapter, we've spent over four hundred pages waiting for the Savior to come at this point. And when He comes, He's introduced by the Father. He then introduces Himself, and then He does one of the most intimate things that He could possibly do. He invites all of those present to come and, as it says, to "come forth unto me, that ye may thrust your hands into my side, and also that ye may feel the prints of the nails in my hands and in my feet, that ye may know"—that ye may know—"that I am the God of Israel, and the God of the whole earth, and have been slain for the sins of the world" (3 Nephi 11:14).... That's why He came; He tells them that's why He came. Before they come and have this extraordinary moment with Him, He tells them the why. He didn't look at them as He might have done and recount their sins. He [essentially] says, "Come, this is me. I have come to take your sins upon me."

ELDER DALE G. RENLUND

Ruth and I had the opportunity to visit the set for filming the Church's production of the Book of Mormon: Another Testament of Jesus Christ videos....

The day we visited, the portrayal of Christ calling His twelve disciples, as recorded in 3 Nephi, was being filmed. I was moved to contemplate how Jesus would have lovingly called His disciples from the

> *The gospel of Jesus Christ is the path of happiness.*

assembled crowd. He knew them, loved them, trusted them. Surprisingly, I had never contemplated what the experience would have been like. This depiction enlightened my understanding, and I received one more spiritual confirmation of the reality of the events told in the Book of Mormon. I know that the gospel of Jesus Christ as taught in 3 Nephi is the path of happiness; ultimately, it is the only path to eternal happiness.

ELDER DIETER F. UCHTDORF

My dear friends, if the Savior were here right now, what would He say to you? I believe He would start by expressing His deep love for you. He might say it with words, but it would also flow so strongly just from His presence that it would be unmistakable. It would be reaching deep into your heart. It would be filling your whole soul. And yet, because we are all weak and imperfect, some concerns might creep into your mind. Of course, the Savior would sense that, and I believe He would assure you with words He has spoken in the scriptures: "Fear not; doubt not. Let not your heart be troubled." I believe Jesus Christ would want you to see, feel, and know that He is your strength. He would want you to see yourself the way He sees you. The Savior would declare that you are a daughter or a son of the Almighty God, and He would assure you that Heavenly Father wants you to inherit all He has. Remember that is your destiny. That is your future. That is your choice.

GOD HAS A *Purpose* FOR *You*

ELDER D. TODD CHRISTOFFERSON

God knows where each of us is. He knows each of us perfectly well. He knows our names. He knows us better than we know ourselves.... God has preserved you to be born in this time so you can be the light to others. I don't know why exactly each of us was born, when we were born, and where we were born, but I'm persuaded—I'm convinced—that God has a reason for each of us.

ELDER NEIL L. ANDERSEN

Each of you has a spiritual destiny. You are on a journey through mortality, with a specific mission to accomplish here on earth unique to you.

... You will face challenges. However, you are a son or daughter of God, made in His image. He made your spirit strong and capable of being resilient to the whirlwinds of life.

... You will have obstacles, delays, trials, temptations, distractions, disappointments, and challenges. There will be mistakes. You may wonder about your future.

Don't be discouraged! You will have moments of hope and faith as doors open and obstacles are overcome. Continue, persist, and above all, believe in Jesus Christ.

Your life is before you, and as you live righteously year after year, I assure you that your experiences will confirm to you again and again that Jesus is the Christ. You can and will find peace. The Savior reminds us, "I will not leave you comfortless: I will come to you" (John 14:18).

ELDER ULISSES SOARES

The Lord gives us talents and special gifts for a specific reason: so we can live in the challenges of today and be victorious. The Savior believes in you. We believe in you. We trust you. Turn your heart to the Savior and practice the things the gospel teaches.

> *The Savior believes in you.*

ELDER DAVID A. BEDNAR

Each member of the Lord's restored Church has a personal and one-by-one ministry to perform with family members, friends, and others of God's children.

In this individualized work of the ministry, the Savior frequently relies upon us to deliver His tender mercies. Sometimes we may be aware of the role we are performing in accomplishing God's purposes; many, and perhaps even most times, we are not.

We are blessed to be instruments through whom tender mercies can be delivered to those in need—because the worth of souls is great in the sight of God.

ELDER RONALD A. RASBAND

Never forget—all of you, never forget—you are in the hands of the Lord. I never could have mapped out my own path. Never. It was like . . . I was a chess piece on a chess board, and the Lord and the Holy Ghost were moving me on that board to the next place the Lord wanted me to be. Now, in my life's experience, I think that applies to all of us, because Heavenly Father is no respecter of persons. He loves every one of you . . . as much as He loves me or any of you. And so He wants us to develop our talents. He wants us to multiply our gifts. He wants us to give Him our very best. And at the end of the day, after we do all of that, leave it in the hands of the Lord.

GOD *Answers* OUR *Prayers* AND GIVES US *Revelation*

ELDER RONALD A. RASBAND

God hears our prayers. He answers the one. By divine design, He directs the details of our lives. He loves each and every one of us so very much. Just as Jesus Christ ministered to those in the Holy Land 2,000 years ago, He does the same for us today, wherever we are.

ELDER PATRICK KEARON

I think the wonderful thing about revelation is it's scattered amongst us. We all have it. If we have particular responsibilities, we'll receive revelation in relation to responsibilities we have. But we all receive revelation.... In terms of being an Apostle, I'm very much still learning, so I don't pretend to know much at all. But I know that I'm much more likely to be receptive to the Spirit when I'm humble. When I'm not thinking about myself. When I'm thinking about others. When I'm open. I'm aware that revelation is much more readily sensed at those times.

> ## ELDER ULISSES SOARES
>
> Revelation from God is not always received at the times or in the ways we might expect.
>
> Sometimes our prayers are answered quickly with the outcome we hope for. Sometimes our prayers are not answered in the way we hope for, yet with time we learn that God had greater blessings prepared for us than we initially anticipated.
>
> When the Lord answers yes to our petitions, it gives confidence. When the answer is no, maybe it is to prevent error. When the Lord withholds an answer, maybe it is to have us grow through faith in Him, obedience to His commandments, and a willingness to act on truth.
>
> Heavenly guidance is a reality, but it is important to understand that it comes in the Lord's way and according to His timetable.

God Answers Our Prayers and Gives Us Revelation

ELDER D. TODD CHRISTOFFERSON

Because of the Internet, artificial intelligence, and other technological innovations, we often expect results or information to be available almost instantly.

Realistically, however, we ought not to expect in this life to know all the answers. Especially in matters of eternal significance, sometimes "the Lord seeth fit to chasten his people; yea, he trieth their patience and their faith" (Mosiah 23:21).

While some answers may come quickly, others are simply not available for the moment because information or evidence is lacking. Please do not suppose, however, that a lack of evidence about something today means that evidence doesn't exist or that it will not be forthcoming in the future.

> *Heavenly guidance is a reality.*

When answers are incomplete or lacking altogether, patient study and patient waiting for new information and discoveries to unfold will often be rewarded with understanding.

Please remember, "Search diligently, pray always, and be believing, and all things shall work together for your good, if ye walk uprightly and remember the covenant wherewith ye have covenanted" (Doctrine and Covenants 90:24).

PRESIDENT HENRY B. EYRING

The Bible Dictionary contains one line that helps me in my prayers. It is this: "Prayer is the act by which the will of the Father and the will of the child are brought into correspondence with each other" (Bible Dictionary, "Prayer").

Like many, my prayers have changed over time and with experience. Since my childhood, I have prayed for blessings from God for others and for myself. Many have been granted. Some have not yet produced the blessings I plead for in faith and in the name of Jesus Christ.

The Savior has helped me as I read this line from the Lord's Prayer. He taught "Thy kingdom come. Thy will be done in earth, as it is in heaven" (Matthew 6:10).

The Savior provided the perfect example in the Garden of Gethsemane as He prayed, saying, "Father, if thou be willing, remove this cup from me: nevertheless not my will, but thine, be done . . . And being in an agony he prayed more earnestly" (Luke 22:42, 44).

God Answers Our Prayers and Gives Us Revelation

When our prayers seem to go unanswered, the Savior's example suggests what to do: keep praying more earnestly.

That is exactly what He did, even to the end of His mortal service.

According to the record, Jesus cried with a loud voice, and prayed, "Father, into thy hands I commend my spirit: and having said thus, he gave up the ghost" (Luke 23:46).

His prayers were answered just as ours can be. He was bound eternally to His Father. The will of the Father was His own.

ELDER QUENTIN L. COOK

My mother was a profound example to me of trusting in the Lord during hard times. . . .

When I was nearly five years old, my mother received word that her younger brother had been killed when the battleship on which he was serving was bombed off the coast of Japan near the end of World War II.

This news was devastating to her. She was very emotional and went into the bedroom. After a while, I peeked into the room to see if she was okay. She was kneeling by the bed in prayer.

A great peace came over me because she had taught me to pray to Heavenly Father and love the Savior. This was typical of the example she always set for me.

Mothers and fathers praying with children may be more important than any other example besides the life and ministry of our Savior Jesus Christ.

PRESIDENT JEFFREY R. HOLLAND

Prayer is an expression of the heart. And we can pray silently. We ought to pray silently. We ought to always have a prayer in our heart. But there is something about saying the words, and for me, saying them out loud. And so I'm reminded to not get by on the cheap, if you will, about prayer.

We need to carve out time, and good time, high priority time when we can say the words. Kneel where possible, be vocal, be out loud, and really have that communication. Individuals who might wait for their evening prayer until 11:30 and they're exhausted and the day has taken its toll, and we get a kind of a half-hearted prayer out before we tumble

> *Prayer is an expression of the heart.*

into bed—I'd say, move that prayer up when we're alert and attentive and can think about it and be powerful. This ought to be high-priority expression. And just managing our life a little better, I think, can lead to that kind of vocal communication with the Lord.

HEAVENLY FATHER *Loves* HIS *Children*

ELDER D. TODD CHRISTOFFERSON

As we seek to develop Christlike attributes and adopt the pure love of Christ to guide our ambition, we should recognize that progress and refinement come over time and with divine help—grace to grace, and grace for grace.

Certainly, we are all clumsy when compared to Jesus Christ. But He still deems us worthy of His attention, love, and help, and with that help, our competence grows. Christ's interest in us is remarkably individual and personal, just as with His friends in the days of His mortal ministry.

He is still with us though unseen. He can still weep with and comfort the Marys who have lost brothers, sisters, parents, spouses, or children. Virtue can still flow out of Him to heal women and men reaching out to touch the hem of His garment. Jesus is not afraid of close friendships.

ELDER PATRICK KEARON

Don't we all need both love and mercy? You know, we make mistakes. You will make mistakes. We all do. But you are blessed with this special kind of love and this special kind of mercy as you live in accordance with the covenants you have made and strive to live up to them and repent when you slip in any way. And know that heaven is not trying to keep you out.

PRESIDENT HENRY B. EYRING

Some of us live in beautiful and peaceful surroundings, yet we experience inner turmoil.

During His mortal ministry, the Savior said, "In the world ye shall have tribulation" (John 16:33). Notwithstanding, He gave this wonderful promise to His disciples: "Peace I leave with you, my peace I give unto you: not as the world giveth, give I unto you. Let not your heart be troubled, neither let it be afraid" (John 14:27). It is a comfort to know that this promise of personal peace continues for all of His faithful disciples today.

> *Heaven is not trying to keep you out.*

You may have seen the miracle of this peace on the face of a disciple of Jesus Christ. Many times, I have seen others experiencing peace and perfect serenity while in the midst of great personal loss, tragedy, and continuing trials.

I felt that peace when I reached out to touch, softly, the beautiful wooden cover on the casket of my wife. A photo of my face at that moment shows me smiling. It was a smile of joy. I felt at that moment that I could see her smile as she was meeting the Savior—and that He was smiling at her....

The Lord keeps his promise: "[My] peace I leave with you, my peace I give unto you" (John 14:27). It is a sure promise to the faithful, worthy, and humble disciples of Jesus Christ, no matter what happens in their lives or the lives of those they love.

ELDER DIETER F. UCHTDORF

No matter your attitude toward God, He will not cease to love you.

How many times will Heavenly Father be patient with you?

More than you can comprehend.

How many times will He forgive you?

More than you feel you deserve.

How often will He nurture and comfort you?

More than you can ever know.

> *There is no end to the grace and mercy of our benevolent God.*

There is no end to the grace and mercy of our benevolent God. No limits to the depth of His love. No barrier to His compassion for His children.

God is not our opposition. He is our mentor. Our guide. Our healer. Our Savior.

His self-admitted purpose and greatest joy is our happiness through immortality and eternal life.

PRESIDENT DALLIN H. OAKS

As Latter-day Saints, many of us—not all of us but many of us—are inclined to insist on "the law" and do so in an unloving way.

I receive many letters from people who are devastated

at the choices being made by someone in their family. As they ask, "What are we to do?," the first thing I always suggest is keep loving them. In the end, that is something you and I can always do.

God's love for His children is an eternal reality, but why does He love us so much, and why do we desire that love? The answer is found in the relationship between God's love and His laws. The love of God does not supersede His laws and His commandments, and the effect of God's laws and commandments does not diminish the purpose and effect of His love.

The Savior Jesus Christ commanded and reminded His followers "that ye love one another; as I have loved you.... By this shall all men know that ye are my disciples, if ye have love one to another" (John 13:34–35), and, "If ye love me, keep my commandments" (John 14:15).

May we remember that the Lord Jesus Christ atoned "for the sins of the world, to bring about the plan of mercy, to appease the demands of justice, that God might be a perfect, just God, and a merciful God also" (Alma 42:15).

FOSTER *Unity* AND *Belonging*

ELDER DAVID A. BEDNAR

How can we develop a greater sense of belonging at church? By serving. Sometimes I find people who say, "Well, the church isn't meeting my needs." I don't want to appear harsh. I don't want to seem unkind. But it's not primarily about me or about you. We are to lose our lives in service to other people. There is such an energy—I find it so energizing when I'm fulfilling the responsibility that I have in the Lord's restored Church. I can recall as a younger man, I didn't necessarily think home teaching was the most exhilarating thing to do. And so I would try, sometimes, to find reasons, "I don't know that I can go." But when I went, it was always one of the most enjoyable parts of my day. Didn't start out that way, but as I was anxiously engaged in fulfilling a responsibility, it was enlivening and energizing.

> *The great plan of salvation is big enough for all of Heavenly Father's children.*

ELDER QUENTIN L. COOK

Let me assure you that if you are married or single, have a large family or a small one, you are still part of the Lord's family. I rejoice that the great plan of salvation is big enough for all of Heavenly Father's children. And how especially grateful I am that God's plan provides a way for family relationships to extend beyond the grave. I testify that when we return to the presence of God, we will be eternally united with those we love most.

ELDER ULISSES SOARES

Have you ever pondered on how the principle of respect for human dignity and equality is demonstrated through the simple way we dress in the house of the Lord? We all come to the temple united in one purpose and filled with the desire to be pure and holy in His holy presence.

Dressed in white, all of us are received by the Lord Himself as His beloved children, men and women of God, progeny of Christ. We are privileged to perform the same

Foster Unity and Belonging

ordinances, make the same covenants, commit ourselves to live higher and holier lives, and receive the same eternal promises.

This universal use of white clothing symbolizes that we are all alike unto God and that in the temple we embrace our identities as children of a loving Heavenly Father.

United in purpose, we see one another with new eyes, and in our oneness, we celebrate our differences as divine children of God.

ELDER DIETER F. UCHTDORF

When I read the scriptures, I'm impressed with how much of the Savior's work has to do with bringing people together. Jews and Gentiles, publicans and fishermen, men and women.

Unity is a powerful testimony of the Savior's influence. Jesus Christ declared that the world would believe in Him when they saw the unity of His servants. Perhaps more people in the world would gain a testimony of Jesus Christ and His Church if they saw more unity among us, His disciples.

The unity we seek is not to have everyone see things

in the same way; it's to have everyone look in the same direction—toward Jesus Christ. It is not our common experiences or background that unites us. It is our common objective. We are one not because of where we've been but where we are striving to go, not because of who we are but who we seek to become.

Of course, our perfect example in seeking unity is our Savior, Jesus Christ. Thanks to His atoning sacrifice, all of God's children may be eternally blessed.

The challenges of establishing the Savior's Church require multiple perspectives, but all of them with an eye single to the glory of Heavenly Father and Jesus Christ.

ELDER D. TODD CHRISTOFFERSON

In The Church of Jesus Christ of Latter-day Saints, we are experiencing two kinds of gatherings: the gathering of Israel into the Church and the gathering together of Church members and friends within our stakes and missions. It is very powerful when members, missionaries, and friends gather together in Christ. . . .

As members of this

> *We help one another stay on the covenant path.*

Foster Unity and Belonging

global community, we have the responsibility and opportunity to watch over one another. We help one another stay on the covenant path.

We are a diverse group from many nations with different backgrounds. The one thing that truly unites us is our faith in Jesus Christ. Ask for the love of Christ as you go about your service in your wards and stakes. Suffer with those who suffer; rejoice with those who rejoice. Share His love as widely and effectively as possible. We're all one in the body of Christ.

Study
THE *Book*
OF *Mormon*

ELDER DALE G. RENLUND

It is a miracle that the Book of Mormon: Another Testament of Jesus Christ came forth, but the real miracle happens when you come to know for yourself that it is true. That is what changes lives. The Book of Mormon has changed my life because of what it has taught me about Jesus Christ. He is my Savior and your Savior, my Redeemer and your Redeemer.

ELDER QUENTIN L. COOK

The Book of Mormon is internally consistent, beautifully written, and contains the answers to life's great questions. It is another testament of Jesus Christ. It contains His commandments and gospel teachings.

Continuously reading and studying this sublime book has strengthened my desire to live God's commandments and has provided me with a strong testimony of the living reality of the Son of God.

ELDER NEIL L. ANDERSEN

Imagine reading these words for the first time:

"I will go and do the things which the Lord hath commanded, for I know that the Lord giveth no commandments unto the children of men, save he shall prepare a way for them that they may accomplish the thing which he commandeth them" (1 Nephi 3:7).

Can you see and feel how powerful they are?

> *The Book of Mormon contains the answers to life's great questions.*

These words—and thousands of others like them in the Book of Mormon—have gone into my heart like a fire. I know they are true. I know they were spoken by a real individual whose name was Nephi.

The truth of the Book of Mormon stands next to the truth of the Bible in assuring us that Jesus is the Christ. Now, in my seventy-fourth year, I love it more than ever.

I hope you can try to remember those feelings you had as you have read this book. The Book of Mormon is the

Study the Book of Mormon

physical manifestation of the truthfulness of the Restoration and of the divine mission of the Prophet Joseph Smith.

Through the power of the Holy Ghost—the truthfulness of the voice of the Spirit—I know that God the Father and His Son, Jesus Christ, appeared to the young Joseph. He was and is a prophet of God, called to restore the gospel and prepare a people to prepare for the return of our Savior Jesus Christ.

He is who we claim him to be. I witness as he did that Jesus is the Christ, the Son of God.

ELDER GARY E. STEVENSON

I give thanks for the powerful influence of the Book of Mormon in my life. This precious book has provided me with many opportunities to learn more about Jesus Christ....

I am grateful for the invitation and promise the Lord has offered to each of us, and to everyone who reads the Book of Mormon, that by the power of the Holy Ghost, we may know of its truthfulness. The truths you read in it will strengthen your faith and fill your soul with light.

DIRECT MESSAGES

ELDER RONALD A. RASBAND

My sincere love for studying the gospel of Jesus Christ in the Book of Mormon started more than fifty years ago as a young missionary for The Church of Jesus Christ of Latter-day Saints. In the five decades since that time, my testimony that the Book of Mormon is the word of God has grown in immeasurable ways.

Since being called to the Quorum of the Twelve Apostles . . . , I have had the distinct pleasure of traveling the world and testifying to people in many countries—from everyday citizens to kings of nations—that the Book of Mormon is "the keystone of our religion, and a man would get nearer to God by abiding by its precepts, than by any other book" (introduction to the Book of Mormon). . . .

I add my witness of the Book of Mormon to the scores of latter-day prophets and apostles who have testified of it before me. The world needs answers to questions of everyday life and of eternal life to come. We all need to know of God's abiding love for us. We need to know that Jesus Christ has provided a way for us to return to our Heavenly Father. This is all included in the Book of Mormon.

ELDER DALE G. RENLUND

In a recent meeting with missionaries I was asked, "What is the Book of Mormon for you?"

To answer, I turn . . . to the introduction to the Book of Mormon. Near the end it reads: "We invite all men everywhere to read the Book of Mormon, to ponder in their hearts the message it contains, and then to ask God, the Eternal Father, in the name of Christ if the book is true. Those who pursue this course and ask in faith will gain a testimony of its truth and divinity by the power of the Holy Ghost."

That's me. That's what the Book of Mormon is to me. I came to know by the power of the Holy Ghost the Book of Mormon is true.

Then the last paragraph reads, "Those who gain this divine witness from the Holy Spirit will also come to know by the same power that Jesus Christ is the Savior of the world, that Joseph Smith is His revelator and prophet in these last days, and that The Church of Jesus Christ of Latter-day Saints is the Lord's kingdom once again established on the earth, preparatory to the Second Coming of the Messiah."

Every aspect of those two paragraphs in the Book of

Mormon introduction applies to me. It is the beginning of how I came to know that Jesus is the Christ. It is the beginning of me knowing about the Church, a beginning of me knowing about Joseph Smith. It is the keystone of my religion. It is the basis of it.

I love the Book of Mormon, and I know a person will come closer to Heavenly Father and Jesus Christ by abiding by its precepts than by any other means. I know this is true for me and it is true for you.

ELDER D. TODD CHRISTOFFERSON

We have an incomparable opportunity to improve our testimony of Jesus Christ with [a study of] the Book of Mormon.

No other scripture so clearly lays out the plan of redemption. No other volume teaches more persuasively the reality and meaning of the Atonement of Jesus Christ. No other part of the scriptural canon possesses the converting power of the Book of Mormon in its witness that Jesus is the Christ and that He has overcome death, both physical and spiritual.

The Book of Mormon is a plain exposition of gospel

Study the Book of Mormon

truth and the joy that is found in following gospel commandments.

> *The Book of Mormon is a plain exposition of gospel truth.*

It is the word of God, and "the virtue of the word of God" (Alma 31:5) is that it produces faith in the Savior—faith that pushes out the doubt, depression, and anxiety that might otherwise overwhelm us, leaving in their place strength and reassurance.

PRESIDENT JEFFREY R. HOLLAND

More than any other one thing, the Book of Mormon gave me my faith, gave me my conviction as a missionary. I should have had it sooner, and maybe you'll have had it sooner or later—and maybe you'll have it a different way—but for me it was the Book of Mormon that bore witness to my very soul, that electrified me in every cell of my body, that this was the word of God and that prophets had died as well as lived to put this into my hands and that it would do more to bring me closer to God as a book than any other book that had been written. And I testify with no reservation and no compromise and not a shadow of retreat from the testimony that the Book of Mormon is true and that Moroni appeared with a set of plates—led the Prophet to a set of plates—and thus comes this volume of scripture.

> *Come and feast on the words of Christ.*

ELDER GERRIT W. GONG

The scriptures invite us to . . . "feast upon the words of Christ; . . . The words of Christ will tell you all things what ye should do" (2 Nephi 32:3).

Come and feast on the words of Christ. The word is not "nibble," it is not "pick at," it is not "tentatively sample." It is "feast"—"feast" as in feel deeply nourished as you savor every bite. Not tentatively but wholeheartedly, come feast on:

- The holy scriptures, especially the Book of Mormon: Another Testament of Jesus Christ
- The words of the prophets and apostles (including general conference)
- Personal prayer
- The holy house of the Lord
- Sabbath worship and classes

Study the Book of Mormon

- The whispering of the Spirit as we minister with love and understanding to each other in sometimes challenging situations
- Honest and authentic expressions and words we share with each other when we speak from our hearts things as they really are, and which really matter, in love

[When] we each have so much for which to be grateful, please feast on the words of the Lord, please come in some way closer to Him each day, and please let your daily patterns, your small and simple things, keep you close to Him.

Learn FROM *Different* PERSPECTIVES

ELDER QUENTIN L. COOK

We come together with distinct cultural, linguistic, and religious backgrounds. Let us appreciate the uniqueness each person, neighbor, and friend offers as the fellow brothers and sisters we truly are.

"Now therefore ye are no more strangers and foreigners, but fellowcitizens with the saints, and of the household of God" (Ephesians 2:19).

ELDER PATRICK KEARON

I would encourage you to take your place in society, in contributing to society. We need to think about Jesus Christ, who's come to do everything for all of us that we cannot do for ourselves. I want to invite you to avoid the extremes in discourse in public life and in private life too. It's very, very hard for two people at opposite poles to see eye to eye when in fact it would do us very well to turn and read and listen to the ideology and thoughts and concepts of those we currently may disagree with. If we'll do that, and do that with an open heart, we'll be blessed to understand those we disagree with and become a force for peace.

> *Let us appreciate the uniqueness each person, neighbor, and friend offers.*

We need to watch, we need to talk to those who don't share our ideas and come to an understanding of them and recognize, step by step by step, that above all else, they are, of course, children of God too. And they want happy lives, and they want happy lives for their children and their grandchildren to be. And you must be examples of this. You have the gospel as your foundation. You have been taught that we must be peacemakers, and this is a work for you to do.

ELDER ULISSES SOARES

Spending time with friends who have different views and trying to understand their perspective offers at least three benefits beyond just enjoying friendship:

1. It strengthens our love and compassion for one another.

Learn from Different Perspectives

2. It broadens our perspective and can lead to greater insight.
3. It helps clarify and strengthen our own beliefs, allowing us to express them more clearly and confidently.

The world would be better and more peaceful if more people joined together and sincerely tried to understand the perspectives of those who think or believe differently. We are all children of God, which makes each of us spiritual brothers and sisters.

ELDER DALE G. RENLUND

[Remember] five gifts we can give each other:
- The gift of tolerance by rejecting hatred.
- The gift of acceptance by rejecting demonizing entire peoples because of the actions of a few.
- The gift of understanding by not judging others solely on outward characteristics.
- The gift of civility and decency by rejecting condemnation, maligning, and vilifying of others who disagree with us.
- The gift of advancing society by respecting all people, especially those who have a different viewpoint.

Covenants
BRING *Power*

ELDER DIETER F. UCHTDORF

In our quest to become our best selves, we willingly take upon ourselves certain constraints. These constraints are sometimes called commandments and covenants. These covenants and commandments are not burdensome. They are delights—for they are the very things that guide you from your current state into the person of glory you wish to become.

PRESIDENT HENRY B. EYRING

I am deeply thankful for the blessings of the restored gospel of Jesus Christ. I am grateful for cleansing power, which is made available to us through His infinite Atonement.

I have felt, as have you, forgiveness and cleansing through baptism by those with authority, and through repenting and partaking of the sacrament. I have felt the burning in the bosom that is only possible because of these words spoken by authorized servants of God: "Receive the Holy Ghost."

ELDER NEIL L. ANDERSEN

The decision to enter the temple for your own endowment and to make sacred covenants is a distinct marker, a transition, a passage in your life that affirms your desire and willingness to God that you consciously take the step to move into spiritual adulthood.

In our ever-changing world, the temple endowment and ordinances help us have a perspective that is timeless and eternal. We learn in the house of the Lord how to best follow Jesus Christ and how to prepare ourselves to live eternally with our Heavenly Father. With the varying views that exist in our world today, the temple endowment allows us to clearly see God's plan for His sons and daughters.

Covenants Bring Power

ELDER GARY E. STEVENSON

Yes, we honor the Lord by building a beautiful structure, as did Solomon in the Old Testament, but we honor Him more by performing the sacred ordinances that only take place in a dedicated house of the Lord.

The temple endowment and ordinances help us have a perspective that is timeless and eternal.

We invite all to come to Jesus Christ and make sacred promises in His temples. The invitation from Jesus Christ is universal:

"Come unto me, all ye that labour and are heavy laden, and I will give you rest.... For my yoke is easy, and my burden is light" [Matthew 11:28, 30].

ELDER DAVID A. BEDNAR

If I had the wish of my heart, I would look into your eyes and I would say: The Lord Jesus Christ made these blessings possible for you individually. You. Not your neighbor, not your spouse. I'm talking to you. Don't deflect it to somebody else. Don't say it doesn't apply to me. I'm talking to you.

... The Savior said, "Come unto me, all ye that labour"—now listen—"and are heavy laden" (Matthew 11:28). He didn't say, "Come unto me, and I will make it smooth." "For my yoke is easy, and my burden is light" (v. 30). Do you realize that through the covenants and the ordinances of the gospel of Jesus Christ that you and I are yoked to and with the resurrected and the living Lord Jesus Christ and His Eternal Father? As we study, learn, understand the covenants of the gospel of Jesus Christ, as we then exercise our moral agency to enter into those covenants, it establishes a connection and a channel with the Father and the Son. And through that covenant channel comes into our lives the power of godliness, strength, capacity, grace beyond our own that doesn't magically make hard things go away, but in the strength of the Lord enables us to do things we could never otherwise do. These promised blessings are for you.

> *These promised blessings are for you.*

CELEBRATE *Christ's* RESURRECTION

ELDER NEIL L. ANDERSEN

The mortal life of Jesus Christ was filled with miracles: a virgin mother, a new star, angels appearing to shepherds, the blind seeing, the lame walking, angels in Gethsemane and at the tomb, and the greatest miracle of all—His glorious Resurrection.

As we learn in the Bible Dictionary, "Christianity is founded on the greatest of all miracles, the Resurrection of our Lord. If that be admitted, other miracles cease to be improbable." (Bible Dictionary, "Miracles").

Jesus Christ's Resurrection truly is miraculous. And because He lives today, we can and should expect miracles to occur in our lives—including the hope of our own glorious resurrection one day.

Because He lives today, we can and should expect miracles to occur.

ELDER D. TODD CHRISTOFFERSON

The Resurrection of Jesus Christ is the proof that He, in fact, possesses power to redeem all who will come unto Him—redeem them from sorrow, injustice, regret, sin, and even death.

Consider for a moment the significance of the Resurrection in resolving once and for all the true identity of Jesus of Nazareth and the great philosophical contests and questions of life. If Jesus was, in fact, literally resurrected, it necessarily follows that He is a divine being. No mere mortal has the power in himself to come to life again after dying.

Because He was resurrected, Jesus cannot have been only a carpenter, a teacher, a rabbi, or a prophet. Because He was resurrected, Jesus had to have been a God, even the Only Begotten Son of the Father.

While we always remember Christ's suffering and death to atone for our sins, at Easter we celebrate the most wonderful of Sundays, the Lord's day, on which He rose from the dead. "For as in Adam all die, even so in Christ shall all be made alive" (1 Corinthians 15:22).

Celebrate Christ's Resurrection

PRESIDENT HENRY B. EYRING

As we celebrate [the] sacred Easter season, let us remember the profound love and sacrifice of our Savior, Jesus Christ. His Resurrection brings hope, renewal, and the promise of eternal life. Through His triumph over death, we are given the assurance that we too can overcome our trials and find everlasting joy.

May we find peace in His teachings and strive to follow His example of compassion and service.

ELDER GARY E. STEVENSON

In the Book of Mormon, we read about the power and Resurrection of Jesus Christ and then two important elements that are part of Easter that come to us through the Resurrection of Jesus Christ and His Atonement. First, a physical restoration, which includes that our body will be restored to the soul, and even a hair of the head shall not be lost to "their proper and perfect frame" (Alma 40:23). And then we think about a spiritual restoration that comes through the Resurrection of Jesus Christ and through His Atonement. The spiritual restoration includes a restoration of everything which is good, righteous, just, merciful [see Alma 41:13], for each one of us. Brigham Young said, "The only true riches in existence [for you and me are] to secure for ourselves a holy resurrection" (*Teachings of Presidents of the Church: Brigham Young* [1997], 277). And so this Easter season, I bear testimony of Jesus Christ. I bear testimony that He is the Son of God. I bear testimony of His literal Resurrection and that which allows the resurrection of all of us as eternal families.

> *His Resurrection brings hope, renewal, and the promise of eternal life.*

PRESIDENT DALLIN H. OAKS

Christmas and Easter are the most public celebrations of Jesus Christ and His ministry. Unfortunately, many Christmas celebrations have increasingly diminished references to the birth of Jesus Christ. Now it is mostly a retail holiday.

For those of us who celebrate Christmas for its true reason, it is easy to understand our celebration of the

Celebrate Christ's Resurrection

birth of the Savior because everyone understands what it means to be born. Easter celebrations do not have that clarity because there is a widespread difference of opinion among various Christian denominations on the meaning of resurrection—literal or symbolic of something difficult to understand.

For Latter-day Saints, the Resurrection means that all who have ever lived will be resurrected. And the Resurrection is literal. As we read in the Book of Mormon, "Now, there is a death which is called a temporal death; and the death of Christ shall loose the bands of this temporal death, that all shall be raised from this temporal death" (Alma 11:42).

Redemption through Jesus Christ is the central message of the prophets of all ages. The books of the New Testament teach that our Savior's suffering and His bloodshed atones for our sins, and that His Resurrection assures that all who have ever lived on this earth will also be resurrected. Then we will all live forever with a glorified body of flesh and bones.

When we understand the vital position of the Resurrection in God's plan of redemption that governs our eternal journey, we see why the Apostle Paul taught,

"If there be no resurrection of the dead, . . . then is our preaching vain, and your faith is also vain" (1 Corinthians 15:13).

. . . Let us prepare for an Easter celebration of the atoning sacrifice of Jesus Christ, culminating in His Resurrection, the most glorious event in history. And this causes us to contemplate our own future resurrection. No matter what others believe or do, we should celebrate the Resurrection of our living Savior by studying His teachings and helping to establish Easter traditions in our society as a whole, especially within our own families. We challenge you to do so.

PRESIDENT RUSSELL M. NELSON

We have all [dealt] with dramatic and unexpected events. Amid such uncertainty, there is only one way to feel at peace—the real peace that passes all understanding. That peace is found in faith in the Lord Jesus Christ. When He suffered for our sins and weaknesses, died on the cross, and rose again, the Savior rewrote human history. Because of Him, we do not have to deal with our frailties, sins and fears alone. Because of Him, death is not the end.

Celebrate Christ's Resurrection

Resurrection will come to all who have ever lived. Because of Him, families can be together forever. Because of Jesus Christ, we celebrate Easter, and Easter is all about peace and hope.

> *The Resurrection means that all who have ever lived will be resurrected.*

On . . . Palm Sunday, I invite you to make this coming week truly holy by remembering not just the palms that were waved to honor the entrance of Jesus into Jerusalem, but by remembering the palms of His hands. According to Isaiah, the Savior promised that He will never forget you, saying, "Behold, I have graven thee upon the palms of my hands" (Isaiah 49:16). Now, after all the Lord Jesus Christ did for you, I invite you to do something this week to follow His teachings. You might make your prayers more earnest. You could forgive someone or help a friend in need. You can start today on a new spiritual quest.

This Easter, I encourage you to focus on the Savior. . . . Jesus Christ lives. As our Resurrected and Atoning Savior, He stands ready to help us grow from the dramatic, unexpected events in our lives. Let us worship and praise Him for the peace, hope, light, and truth He brings to us.

ELDER GERRIT W. GONG

We live in a world which is isolated or lonely sometimes. And I think the Lord's saying, "Wherever you are, whatever your circumstance, I want you to feel my love." It's the way that we can answer all the longings of our hearts. Everything that we experience, He understands. He came to succor us according to the flesh, because He understands everything in love. And that's what Easter is. And its why Easter is important. Because He lives. I remember [a father] whose daughter had died in the sparkle of her life. He put his arms around me and said, "I would give anything to see her again." And he wept, and I wept. And what a blessing to assure this father that he will see his daughter and they'll be reunited as a family. We can be the richest of all people, for we can have the riches of eternity. That's His promise.

ELDER DALE G. RENLUND

Ruth and I [once] escorted a group of clergy through [a temple open house]. They admired a painting depicting the risen Lord and asked, "Do you believe that the Resurrection of Jesus Christ was literal?" Our answer was an emphatic, "Yes! We absolutely do."

Not only was the Resurrection literal for Jesus Christ, but it will be literal for everyone who has ever lived or will live on the earth. [During the] Easter season, we rejoice in the hope of this universal gift that God gives to all of us.

PRESIDENT JEFFREY R. HOLLAND

When Christ is resurrected, the verses from John [chapter 20] that are recorded that caught my eye are about Mary—first of all, Mary Magdalene. "She runneth, and cometh to Simon Peter, and to the other disciple, whom Jesus loved, and saith unto them, They have taken away the Lord out of the sepulchre, and we know not where they have laid him" (John 20:2) And that's verse two. Verse four: "So they ran both together: and the other disciple did outrun Peter, and came first to the sepulchre." That's John's account. Here's a parallel verse or two from Matthew [28:2, 6–8]:

"[It] was a great earthquake: for the angel of the Lord descended from heaven, and came and rolled back the stone from the door, and sat upon it." And when they ask, the angel says, "He is not here: for he is risen." And then, in response, "And go quickly, and tell his disciples that he is risen from the dead; and, behold, he goeth before you into Galilee; there shall ye see him: lo, I have told you. And they departed quickly from the sepulchre with fear and great joy; and did run to bring his disciples word."

Mary Magdalene running, Peter and John running, the angel telling them to run again and to go quickly. And they depart quickly, and they did run. This is a message worth running for. This is a message worth being quick for departure and quick for service. I love missionaries who run from door to door, and I've seen bishops who run from house to house. I've seen Relief Society presidents who run from sister to sister. I'm grateful for that kind of devotion in the gospel of Jesus Christ. It's worth running and telling the world that He has risen.

ELDER GARY E. STEVENSON

I find with great interest that one of the greatest Easter stories that has ever been told is one that comes to us through the Book of Mormon. Consider Jesus Christ, a resurrected being now, as part of His Easter ministry,

Celebrate Christ's Resurrection

visiting the people of the Book of Mormon. Here we read in the Book of Mormon in 3 Nephi [11:15–17], "And it came to pass that the multitude went forth ... and did feel the prints of the nails in his hands and in his feet; ... going forth one by one until they did see with their eyes and did feel with their hands, and did know of a surety and did bear record, that it was he.... [And] they did cry out ..., saying: Hosanna! Blessed be the name of the Most High God! And they did fall down at the feet of Jesus, and did worship him."

> *Everything that we experience, He understands.*

What a beautiful Easter story that comes to us through the restored gospel of Jesus Christ, the Book of Mormon.

PURSUE *Education* AND LIFELONG *Learning*

ELDER RONALD A. RASBAND

My feeling about observation is we can learn something from everybody that we come in contact with. And if you develop a mindset that you can always be taught, that you can always learn something, it doesn't matter if the person is cleaning my office at the end of the day. If I get into a conversation with that person, I have tried to train my mind and my heart [to ask], What, maybe, could I learn from this person? And if we have willing spirits that are always humble enough to admit that we can learn something from every one of Heavenly Father's children and not be so prideful to think that we have all the answers, this great capability of learning through observation can be a lifelong journey.

> *Learning through observation can be a lifelong journey.*

DIRECT MESSAGES

ELDER D. TODD CHRISTOFFERSON

Lifelong learning needs to involve lifelong spiritual learning, not only intellectual or training in a trade. It's lifelong learning of the gospel of Jesus Christ. And you can't get to the bottom of all there is in the richness of the gospel in one life. So don't worry about running out of opportunities to study in the scriptures and know what the Lord is like and what you can become.

ELDER ULISSES SOARES

I invite you to consider the following concepts ... as you work to accomplish challenging tasks in your own life:

- Strengthen your belief that the Lord is accomplishing a great work through you.
- Ask for God's help through sincere prayer for ways to accomplish what He is asking you to do.
- Show diligence by studying, working, and practicing.
- Understand the importance of being worthy of the companionship of the Holy Ghost by keeping the commandments and living the commandments.

Pursue Education and Lifelong Learning

- Purify your motives by loving God and by loving His children and desiring to bless them.

I promise that emphasizing these principles will help you to accomplish the work that your Heavenly Father has given you.

ELDER RONALD A. RASBAND

If a young and busy college student were to come to me to ask for advice about his or her studies, my answer would be simple:

Give the Lord equal time.

You might be thinking: "I just do not have time, Elder Rasband. I am already over-committed; I have to get good grades; I am taking too many credit hours; I have tough professors who expect my full attention; I am working and I can barely get to church on Sunday."

Know this: you cannot put your testimony on the shelf during your college years. Give the Lord equal time in your university experience, then give Him equal time the rest of your life.

I promise you this: as you give the Lord equal time in the pursuit of higher learning, the Spirit will enhance your academic pursuits, you will find you have extra time and capacity for your courses, and doors will be opened for you that might have otherwise been closed.

ELDER D. TODD CHRISTOFFERSON

Some people go into professions, some people go into the military. Some people go into the arts. Some people go into the vocations and the crafts and the trades and all of those are excellent choices. It's just that we need to grow from where we are as young people, as youth, and continue, as President Nelson talks about, in lifelong learning.

> *Give the Lord equal time.*

We have to prepare ourselves. We need to prepare ourselves. It's a religious obligation, he said, so that we can be of service to other people. It's not just for our own edification, our own income. Those things matter, but really we want to be of service in society, in the Church, and in the broader society. So I want to emphasize there's no one profession, no one occupation, no one training that's best for 100% of all of us. But each of us chooses a path, and ... we can change it as we go along and we learn. You're not expected ... to know

Pursue Education and Lifelong Learning

everything at the beginning. You don't see the end from the beginning. And sometimes it's just, "'Give [me] this day [my] daily bread' [Matthew 6:11]. I need this day, and I'll move to that step and then see where we go after that." But that's okay. You don't have to know it all.

Women HAVE *Influence* AND *Power*

PRESIDENT HENRY B. EYRING

While I do not fully know all the Lord's purposes in giving the primary responsibility for nurturing to faithful sisters, I believe it is because of their divine capacity to love. To love in such a way that the needs of others are felt more deeply than their own—that is charity. That is the pure love of Christ.

... I express heartfelt gratitude to the mothers who love with Christlike charity, who strengthen faith and who build the rising generation with hope and tenderness. You are the heart of the Lord's work.

ELDER QUENTIN L. COOK

In the world today, there are enormous forces arrayed against women and families. We recognize that women are confronted with many options and decisions regarding family life, career prospects, and many other good and noble

> *You are the heart of the Lord's work.*

pursuits. How grateful I am for the good women in my life who have allowed their faith in God and in His plan to direct their paths.

My appreciation for all the women who have been a positive influence on me is beyond my ability to adequately communicate. I feel a great responsibility to live up to the example of the women in my life and their noble and vital role in God's eternal plan of happiness for His children.

PRESIDENT RUSSELL M. NELSON

Regardless of your situation, I invite every woman to consider the remarkable relationship that the Lord Jesus Christ had with His mother, Mary.

Repeatedly the Savior gave her special care and attention. Consider just three examples from His life and teachings.

The first miracle Jesus Christ performed during His mortal ministry began with a request from His mother during a family gathering. His eager response signaled his love and respect: "What wilt thou have me to do for thee? that will I do" (Joseph Smith Translation, John 2:4).

Women Have Influence and Power

The second example came at the most poignant time in the Savior's mortal life. As he suffered unspeakable pain on the cross, Jesus focused His compassion on the well-being of His mother. Looking down to His Apostle John standing next to Mary, He said, "Behold thy mother!" [John 19:26]. His meaning was clear: John was to care for Mary.

Finally, consider the way the Savior compared His concern for His wayward brothers and sisters to that of a mother. "How [oft] would I have gathered thy children together, even as a hen gathereth her chickens under her wings" [Matthew 23:37]. When a mother pleads with the Lord on behalf of a struggling child, she does so knowing that the Savior understands perfectly what she is feeling.

> *Every woman is in a position to help build and change lives.*

I am deeply grateful for the remarkable women in my life who have enriched and mothered me, my family, and countless others in life-changing ways. Every woman has within her the essence of motherhood. Every woman is in a position to help build and change lives. May you each know that our Heavenly Father and His Beloved Son know you, see you, and love you.

PRESIDENT JEFFREY R. HOLLAND

To mothers everywhere who sacrifice for their family, I wish to say ... that your sacrifice is not unnoticed—not by the leaders of the Church and not by our Father in Heaven who seeks always the care of His children.

When this earthly chapter of our lives is over and all of the honors of the world have faded away, I believe it may well be righteous mothers who first hear the words, "Well done, thou good and faithful servant: ... enter thou into [my rest]" (Matthew 25:21).

ELDER DAVID A. BEDNAR

I want to link a teaching of the Savior to our recognition of the role of our mothers and the women we love in our lives. The Savior taught that we should learn of Him, walk in the meekness of His Spirit. I'd like us to consider that in the second chapter of John there's an account of a wedding feast, and the mother of Jesus was there. She was the one who indicated that there was a lack of wine. And

Women Have Influence and Power

we all know that the first public miracle of the Savior was the changing of water into wine at that marriage feast. It's interesting to me that that invitation by his mother created the opportunity for the Savior to first disclose His mortal purpose and mission. Ordinary water transformed into something much different and, recognized by the guests of the feast, much better. That's the very purpose of the Savior. Through Him, through His Atonement, through His Resurrection, we are transformed from natural men and women into men and women of Christ, much better than we otherwise could ever be. That was the beginning of the Savior's ministry—responding to the invitation of his mother. That's how his ministry began.

At the end of his ministry, hanging on the cross, He points to His mother, and He calls her "woman" [John 19:26]. As I understand it, in the culture and language of the time, that's one of the ultimate compliments: Woman. Woman of all women, the greatest of all. And then He lovingly makes sure the disciple will make sure that His mother is cared for. The mother of Jesus played a foundational role at the beginning of His ministry, His public ministry. She was there at the cross, and He demonstrated His reverence and love for her. As we follow His example, we'll show that same kind of love and reverence for the mothers and the women in our lives that mean so much to us.

ELDER DIETER F. UCHTDORF

My dear sisters, you hold a special place in our Father's plan for the eternal happiness and well-being of His children. Whatever your place is in the sequence of life, you have an important role in the plan of salvation. And God has given you special spiritual gifts, promises, and blessings as daughters of the Creator of the universe.

> *Never underestimate the power of your example and influence.*

Never underestimate the power of your example and influence for good as you serve in your families, communities, and Church callings. Let me assure you that the Lord knows you. He loves you. He will bless you for your dedication to Him and His children.

Family is *Essential*

ELDER ULISSES SOARES

I encourage you to take part in opportunities to strengthen your relationship with those you love. Our family has made countless memories around the dinner table, for example. We love to cook and share meals together, which becomes hours spent in love and support for one another.

Make new memories that fortify your family. Start a new tradition everyone will enjoy. Because families are so central to God's plan, these moments are very important to Him, and we should strive to have them often.

ELDER QUENTIN L. COOK

If you'll do three things, you can be protected and you can protect your families. My wife Mary and I, in our 20s, we had moved to [the] San Francisco [area]. I attended law school there and was practicing law, and we were beginning to raise our family. And it was a period where there was much social unrest, like there is in the world today. The Vietnam War was going on. There was a drug culture. There was a great President of the Quorum of the Twelve that came out and gave us a talk that has stayed with me all these years. And he said, "No matter where you live, no matter whether you're in the minority, if you'll do three things, you can be protected and you can protect your families." And the first one was to build Zion in your hearts and in your homes. And it's interesting because he was talking about religious observance, prayer, family scripture study, love and kindness in the home, not criticizing children. The second one was to be an example, to be a pillar, to be a light on the hill, to allow your own feelings about what's right and wrong, and your own beliefs about the Savior to be exemplified in who you are, the way you live, and the kindness you demonstrate to other people. The third one was to focus on the principles and the covenants that are taught in the temple and make those covenants and getting closer to our Father in Heaven and to Jesus Christ, your

> *The family is God's creation, not a human invention.*

main objective in life. And I came away feeling that, that if you do those three things, you can live anywhere and have the blessings of the gospel.

ELDER GERRIT W. GONG

Fathers are a gift from God. My father, who served many years as a patriarch in the Church, was a spiritual and compassionate man and a wonderful father.

I know some of us have limited relationships with our fathers—often through no fault of our own. Some fathers are absent. Or there may be other reasons relating to fathers that may make a day honoring fathers difficult for you.

Regardless of our relationship with our earthly father, each of us has a Heavenly Father. He knows us by name and loves us individually. Please always remember that you can turn to Him for comfort. Our Heavenly Father loves you eternally and will always be there for you.

ELDER RONALD A. RASBAND

My father taught me what work is by his example. My mother taught me about work by having me do it. . . .

My father was a truck driver, and he would get up very early in the morning, and he'd come home late in the evening, and he just worked, worked, worked. And so from my youngest memories of Dad, it's just of his tenacity going to work every day. And it wasn't a glamorous job. He drove a bread truck, and he had a route, and he went and delivered bread to grocery stores. And there were times I went with him and carried trays of Wonder Bread and Twinkies into grocery stores and just learned from my father the principle of working by observing him and watching him.

Well, from my mother—she didn't give me a pass on learning how to work personally. And she was the taskmaster of our family, and she's the one that kept me busy doing it. And I thought of how an application of that could be applied for all of you.... And I think it's encompassed in three words: "example" and "do it." And I've always felt that whether you're in an employment, like the people I used to lead at Huntsman all around the world, or in Church callings or even a father at home, a leader always has to be an example to be on higher ground so that simply you can just lift people themselves to higher ground. And I think example—beyond the words you're going to use, beyond the talk, is your example.

ELDER D. TODD CHRISTOFFERSON

The family is God's creation, not a human invention. Our loving Father in Heaven sends His children to earth in families because this is an essential part of His plan for our growth, improvement, and happiness. It is strong families that make strong societies. . . .

The day-to-day activities that families do together give children the opportunity to see parents putting into practice the moral values they have taught. They see how those values find expression in—and even define—everyday life. This constant, consistent example communicates more powerfully than any sermon, planting true principles deep into the heart.

The families we form and nurture here on earth are but imperfect imitations of God's heavenly family. His purpose is for us to find joy here and to prepare ourselves for everlasting joy with Him in the hereafter, where the pattern of families continues eternally.

DIRECT MESSAGES

ELDER DIETER F. UCHTDORF

Although the early years of my life were challenging because of the war and its associated worries, I was tremendously blessed to be part of a family that loved me. I was reminded of these early years when Harriet and I visited the home I lived in when I was born as well as the home I lived in as a young child.

During these early years, my family had not yet been introduced to the restored gospel of Jesus Christ. It was a very hard time. Yet I still have some happy memories of these locations because of the love of family, friends, and neighbors.

> *Focus on raising your children with Christlike love.*

Perhaps some of you parents (or those who will one day be parents) are concerned about the world into which you are bringing your children. Might I suggest that if you focus on raising your children with Christlike love and teaching them to love our Father in Heaven and Savior Jesus Christ, they will be empowered with the ability to navigate through all of life's challenges. They will be able to feel the joy and peace that comes from living the Savior's gospel despite difficulties.

Disciples FOLLOW *Christ's* EXAMPLE

ELDER ULISSES SOARES

Let me say that following the Savior is always the answer to life's questions. The Savior's heart is full of mercy. He is always ready to help and succor us. As we draw closer to Him and surrender ourselves spiritually to His care, He can make our burdens light. I pray you can see your trials through the eyes of faith, and not give up.

Whatever your question may be, know that the Lord hears you and is walking with you. As you then walk with Him, He blesses you with His Spirit, helping you to see things clearly, and He fills you with His love.

ELDER PATRICK KEARON

The Savior, the Good Shepherd, goes in search of His lost sheep until He finds them. He is "not willing that any should perish" (2 Peter 3:9).

Let us follow His example and respond to the impressions we receive, no matter how insignificant they may seem. Let us ask our Father in Heaven what we might do, and for whom, and do it.

PRESIDENT DALLIN H. OAKS

The only role model we are safe to follow *overall* is that of our Savior. His example and teachings define the path for every disciple of Jesus Christ. Following Christ is not a casual or occasional practice but a continuous commitment and way of life that applies at all times and in all places.

Study the life of our Lord and Savior Jesus Christ and make His qualities your role model for mortality and all eternity. Disciples of Christ seek to follow Him and become like Him, not only here but also hereafter.

ELDER D. TODD CHRISTOFFERSON

Occasionally I encounter someone who feels that he or she must lay aside religion to excel in their profession or

Disciples Follow Christ's Example

whatever they are passionate about in life. In their view, matters of faith are a distraction or, even worse, a handicap in pursuing the achievements they seek.

I believe that just the opposite is true. It is centering our lives in Jesus Christ that leads to excellence. Christian discipleship is the path to achievement. Christ is not an obstacle but the key to success in all that really matters.

The Savior's qualities are the virtues and character traits that are foundational to success in any arena and any enterprise, including marriage and family life. Whether it be science, law, business, art, social work, parenting, or any other pursuit in life, these are the qualities that permit a person to excel. They bear the fruit of capability and productivity in life.

> *It is centering our lives in Jesus Christ that leads to excellence.*

Ultimately, centering our lives in Jesus Christ leads to excellence. With your life centered in Christ, you will be living evidence of what His influence and grace can achieve in a disciple.

WE CAN *Repent* AND WE CAN *Forgive*

ELDER NEIL L. ANDERSEN

Wherever we are on our journey through life, as disciples of the Lord Jesus Christ we constantly treasure the blessing to repent. Repentance is not punishment; repentance is a redemptive gift from a loving Heavenly Father.

With open arms, our Savior bids us, "Come unto me" (Matthew 11:28). If you find yourself temporarily facing setbacks, don't become discouraged; focus on your love of the Savior and His love for you! ... Week by week, we can repent and become better because of Jesus Christ.

ELDER QUENTIN L. COOK

One of the reasons that the Savior's Atonement is not appreciated in the world at large is because much of society takes the position that a loving Father in Heaven should exact no consequences for conduct that is contrary to His commandments.

This was apparently the position taken by Corianton, the son of Alma the Younger in the Book of Mormon. He had engaged in grievous immoral conduct and was being counseled by Alma.

Alma helped Corianton understand that it is not an "injustice that the sinner should be consigned to a state of misery" (Alma 42:1). He noted that starting with Adam, a merciful God had provided a "space for repentance," because without repentance, "the great plan of salvation would have been frustrated" (Alma 42:5).

Seen in their true light, the glorious blessings of repentance and adherence to the Savior's teachings are monumentally important. It is not unfair to be clear, as Alma was with Corianton, about the consequences of sinful choices and lack of repentance.

> *Through repentance, sinful conduct is blotted out.*

After Corianton's repentance, Alma concluded, "let these things trouble you no more, and only let your sins trouble you, with that trouble which shall bring you down unto repentance" (Alma 42:29).

We Can Repent and We Can Forgive

The remarkable and celestial blessing of the Savior's Atonement is that through repentance, sinful conduct is blotted out.

ELDER D. TODD CHRISTOFFERSON

I've been thinking about the precious gift of repentance. Jesus Christ paid a terrible price so that He could offer us this gift. He could atone for our sins and offer us forgiveness and sanctification. I hear from time to time the phrase, "It's never too late to repent." On the other hand, I would say it's more accurate to say it's not too late to repent. The scriptures tell us that it could be too late, or it can *become* too late. . . . They tell us not to procrastinate, "lest . . . in an hour when you think not the summer shall be past, and the harvest ended, and your souls not saved" [Doctrine and Covenants 45:2]. So I think everyone who's hearing this message, for any of us, it's not too late. But let's not procrastinate, because someday it could be too late. I think this is what President Nelson has in mind when he talks about daily repentance. Not that we keep repenting of the same thing over and over again, but that we make these corrections, usually small course corrections, each day, as we seek to grow in our discipleship. I say again, what a precious gift is repentance.

ELDER DAVID A. BEDNAR

Most of us think that repentance and being without sin is the purpose of mortality. It is not. It is to incrementally, line upon line, precept upon precept, with God's help, through the enabling power of the Savior's Atonement, to become more like Them. "Who shall ascend into the hill of the Lord? ... He who hath clean hands, and a pure heart" [Psalm 24:3–4].

Can you have clean hands and not have a pure heart? Yes. Ultimately, we have to have both. The gospel of Jesus Christ, the Savior's atoning sacrifice, makes possible cleansing from sin when we do things wrong. All of you having entered into covenants or about to enter into covenants with God to receive those promised blessings, ... we are to be good boys, good girls, filling our life with love, service, and devotion to the Savior and to our brothers and sisters. That's why we have moral agency. So being cleansed is absolutely essential, but it's not enough. That's the clean hands. You don't get a pure heart just by trying hard. God has to work in you and on you to help that to occur. That transforming power only comes from Him. So the enabling power of Jesus Christ is the cleansing and the strengthening, just like the people of Alma [see Mosiah 24:15], to do things that in our limited moral capacity we could never do.

PRESIDENT RUSSELL M. NELSON

How is it possible in His time of excruciating agony for Jesus Christ to ask His Father to forgive His tormentors? And yet, on the cross, Jesus did exactly that. He practiced what He had preached. He taught us to love our enemies, to do good to those who hate us, and even to pray for those who despitefully use us. I know from firsthand experiences that forgiveness blesses both the forgiver and the forgiven.

Three children born to Ruth and Jimmy Hatfield suffered from congenital heart disease. They sought my help as a heart surgeon for their two daughters, Laural Ann and Gay Lynn. I was heartbroken when both girls died after I had operated on them. Understandably, Ruth and Jimmy were shattered. And they blamed me. For almost six decades, I was haunted by this situation. I grieved for the Hatfields and tried to establish contact with them several times, but without success. A few years ago, I reached out again to the Hatfield family. Much to my relief, this time, they were willing to meet with me. On bended knee, I poured out my heart to them. The Spirit of the Lord prevailed. They forgave me. And it proved to be a turning point in their lives and in mine. Now I treasure the friendship I share with the Hatfields.

Just think about their courage and humility! They were willing to let go of old hurts. The Spirit of forgiveness released them from burdens they had carried for nearly sixty years. There is nothing easy about forgiving those who have disappointed us, hurt us, cheated us, or spread false rumors about us. However, not forgiving others is poison for us. Grudges weigh us down. Angry disagreements separate us. Animosity and hatred can divide families. And yet, the Savior's counsel is clear: "If ye forgive men their trespasses, your heavenly Father will also forgive you" [Matthew 6:14].

Forgiving others does not mean condoning sinful or criminal behavior. And it certainly does not mean staying in abusive situations. But, when we choose to forgive others, we allow the Lord to remove the poison from our souls. We permit Him to soothe and soften our hearts so we can see others, especially those who have wronged us, as children of God and as our brothers and sisters.

We Can Repent and We Can Forgive

... My dear friends, I invite you prayerfully to consider if there is someone whom you should forgive. Will you free yourself from a grudge you may be harboring? ... I promise that as you forgive, the Savior will relieve you of anger, resentment, and pain. The Prince of Peace will bring you peace. Jesus Christ is risen! He loves you! And because of Him, you can experience the joy and miracle of forgiveness.

ELDER GERRIT W. GONG

As the Golden Rule teaches in Matthew 7, a sanctifying symmetry in repentance and forgiveness invites us each to offer others that which we ourselves need and desire. Sometimes, our willingness to forgive someone else enables both them and us to believe we can repent and be forgiven. Our Savior is our mediator with God. But He also helps bring us to ourselves and each other as we come to Him. Heaven can give us strength and wisdom beyond our own—to know when to hold on and how to let go. We are less alone when we realize we are not alone. Our Savior always understands.

DIRECT MESSAGES

PRESIDENT JEFFREY R. HOLLAND

I've been working in the New Testament a little in my personal study, in addition to *Come, Follow Me*, and I find these virtues in the Savior that I love, that I want to emulate. Some of them are challenging. Well, they're all challenging, but I'm motivated by them. I'm thrilled by them. I am grateful for them. And one of them that I'm grateful for is that He forgets our mistakes. He forgets our falling short, and I'm grateful for that. And just one example . . . : In the midst of His arrest and what would go on to his trials and Crucifixion, it says, . . . "All this was done, that the scriptures of the prophets might be fulfilled. Then all the disciples forsook him, and fled." Right when He needs them the most. All the disciples forsook him and fled. But that's Matthew 26, verse 56. But in Matthew 28[:9–10], when the trials and Crucifixion and terrible, terrible suffering is over [it says], "They went to tell his disciples, [but] behold, Jesus met them, saying, All hail. And they came and held him by the feet, and worshipped him. [And] said Jesus unto them, Be not afraid: go tell my

> *Heaven can give us strength and wisdom beyond our own.*

brethren that they [shall] go into Galilee, and there [they shall] see me." He doesn't say a word about their fleeing. He doesn't say a word about their betrayals. He doesn't say anything about the cock crowing. He just says, "All hail. Glad you're here, and we're going to be happy and head for the Galilee. And we got missions to talk about." I love that willingness to say that "I forgive and forget, and you forget, and let's be happy and keep going." I love that.

GIVE *Thanks* IN *All* THINGS

PRESIDENT DALLIN H. OAKS

When we give thanks in all things, we see hardships and adversities in the context of the purpose of life. We are sent here to be tested. There must be opposition in all things. We are meant to learn and grow through that opposition, through meeting our challenges, and through teaching others to do the same.

When we understand the principle that God offers us opportunities for blessings and blesses us through our own adversities and the adversities of others, we can understand why He has commanded us again and again to "thank the Lord thy God in all things" (Doctrine and Covenants 59:7).

PRESIDENT RUSSELL M. NELSON

There is no medication or operation that can fix the many spiritual woes and maladies that we face.

There is, however, a remedy—one that may seem surprising—because it flies in the face of our natural intuitions. Nevertheless, its effects have been validated by scientists as well as men and women of faith.

I am referring to the healing power of gratitude....

> *Being thankful in all things is both a commandment from the Lord and a spiritual gift.*

Jesus Christ frequently expressed gratitude. Before raising Lazarus from the dead, before miraculously multiplying loaves and fishes, and before passing the cup to His disciples at the Last Supper, the Savior prayed and gave thanks to God. No wonder the Apostle Paul later declared, "In every thing give thanks" [1 Thessalonians 5:18].

Over my nine and a half decades of life, I have concluded that counting our blessings is far better than recounting our problems. No matter our situation, showing gratitude for our privileges is a fast-acting and long-lasting spiritual prescription.

Does gratitude spare us from sorrow, sadness, grief, and pain? No, but it does soothe our feelings. It provides us with a greater perspective on the very purpose and joy of life....

We can all give thanks for the beauties of the earth and

the majesty of the heavens that give us an inkling of the vastness of eternity.

We can give thanks for the gift of life, for our amazing bodies and minds that allow us to grow and learn.

We can give thanks for art, literature, and music that nurture our souls.

We can give thanks for the opportunity to repent, start over, make amends, and build character.

We can give thanks for our families, friends, and loved ones.

We can give thanks for the opportunity to help, cherish, and serve one another, which makes life so much more meaningful.

We can even give thanks for our trials, from which we learn things we would not know otherwise.

Most of all, we can give thanks unto God, the Father of our spirits, which makes us all brothers and sisters—one great global family.

ELDER NEIL L. ANDERSEN

Being thankful in all things is both a commandment from the Lord and a spiritual gift we can inherit. The admonition to both give thanks unto God for whatsoever blessing you are blessed with, and to love the Lord thy God with all thy heart, and with all thy soul, and with all thy mind, invites us to make gratitude and thanksgiving qualities planted deep inside our character. In life, we experience struggles, disappointments, and challenges of all kinds. It can be difficult to be grateful during these moments, but there is hope in Jesus Christ. With faith in our Savior, we triumph over sin, temptations, unfairness, and the challenges of this mortal life. Knowing we have a Savior who loves us through all the seasons of our life brings us comfort and peace. Our final destination isn't here on Earth, but in the presence of our Father in Heaven and His Son, Jesus Christ. I am so grateful for the hope we have in Jesus Christ. He is our hope and our promise. I express with you our gratitude to Heavenly Father for the gift of His Beloved Son. I know He lives.

ELDER D. TODD CHRISTOFFERSON

Whatever we may lack, we still gratefully acknowledge the multitude of blessings we have already received at the Lord's hand. A friend recently wrote about learning a traditional song from the Jewish Passover celebration called, "It Would Have Been Enough." The song recounts Israel's deliverance from Egypt and divine blessings and interventions, any one which "would have been enough." For example, "If God had only given us manna, it would have been enough, but He also gave us the sabbath."

We could sing, "If God had only given us the Book of Mormon, it would have been enough, but He also gave us the Doctrine and Covenants and the Pearl of Great Price." Or, "If God had only given us a temple for every continent, it would have been enough, but now He gives us holy temples in our own nations."

> *As you pray, express gratitude.*

Our Heavenly Father indeed grants blessing upon blessing. That is a message from the Spirit that applies to each of us. I do believe that the Lord has more to give for those who feel and express gratitude for what they have already received. I pray that all of us will have hearts that overflow with gratitude to God, especially for the gift of His Son, Jesus Christ, whose atoning sacrifice and Resurrection bring to each of us the incomparable blessings of immortality and eternal life.

DIRECT MESSAGES

PRESIDENT JEFFREY R. HOLLAND

Despite the numerous challenges that have presented themselves over the last year and a half in my life, it is because of the gifts from Jesus Christ that I can remain grateful and optimistic about the future.

I am grateful for the promise of enjoying eternal life with the ones I love, made possible because of Christ's infinite atoning sacrifice. Likewise, I am eternally grateful for the supplication of thousands of people who repeatedly sought heaven's intervention in my behalf during my months of illness and loss.

I am grateful for the women of the Church who have been as strong as Mount Sinai and as compassionate as the Mount of Beatitudes. I am thankful for the Church's army of teachers, officers, advisers, and clerks, to say nothing of people who are forever setting up tables and taking down chairs.

Too often I have failed to express gratitude for the faith and goodness of these people in my life. My thanks be to all you wonderful members of The Church of Jesus Christ of Latter-day Saints—and legions of good people not of our faith—for proving every day of your life that the pure love of Christ "never faileth" (1 Corinthians 13:8).

Give Thanks in All Things

Although I do not yet qualify, I am forever thankful to my Savior for all He has done and continues to do for me. How grateful I am for the promise that everyone "who receiveth all things with thankfulness shall be made glorious" (Doctrine and Covenants 78:19).

ELDER DAVID A. BEDNAR

As you pray, express gratitude. . . . Offer a prayer—not every time, but occasionally—and don't ask for anything, just express gratitude. You'll be amazed what the Holy Ghost will teach you in your prayers when you're not focused on you and what you want.

WORK

TOWARD

Worthy

Goals

ELDER GERRIT W. GONG

The expression "bloom where you're planted" has always been true—but perhaps it is especially true now. This phrase symbolizes faith and flexibility....

One of the things which has been most tender to me about this unique time is that I have experienced this season in a different way this year. Because I have not been traveling on Church assignments, I have learned to garden with my wife. When I am in the garden with her, I grow in love for gardens and for her. I've gotten to smell the flowers and hear the birds in a different way.

There is so much for each of us to learn and experience in situations like this. Many of us have learned to use technology in new ways to communicate with others. There are new patterns, new ways to think about what it means to be connected. I hope we will remember the lessons we had here and will remember to cherish the time we had together and the time not rushing around.

DIRECT MESSAGES

I testify that the Father and the Son are in the details of our lives. Sometimes we may feel alone, lost, isolated, or separate, but we are not. We should always remember our Lord Jesus Christ knows us. He loves us. And we are never lost to Him. He is aware of us in the darkest hours and in the brightest days. With His help, we can truly learn to bloom where we are planted.

> *With His help, we can truly learn to bloom where we are planted.*

ELDER PATRICK KEARON

One of my fears for you is that you had this mission experience and now what happens is that you might go back to where you were. Now, you might go back to where you were physically. You might go back to where the family was and is. You might do that, but do not—don't dare to go back to where you were in your head and your heart before your mission. That would be like an army in retreat. As a foe advances towards you, you're turning and running away. . . . You must not go back to where you were. And some of you have already felt yourself slipping in that direction, and you've got frightened already because you've seen and felt this happening as you've gone, as you've slipped backwards. I'm here to plead with you not to fall for that.... Do I understand that there are forces that pull you down? Yes, I do. Do I understand that you are in a frightening or potentially frightening moment? Yes, I certainly do. And we do. And we plead for you to keep reaching up. Why? Well, that is what your Father in Heaven wants. And that is what His Son, Jesus Christ, wants for you.

ELDER GARY E. STEVENSON

The Daruma doll is a cherished symbol in Japanese culture of good luck and perseverance. It is used to set goals and celebrate achievement and success. When someone commits to a goal, they color in an eye and ask for divine assistance to achieve it. After the goal is achieved, they color in the other as a sign of gratitude.

While our ... goals may include ways to improve physically or temporally, I encourage you to counsel with your Father in Heaven and also set meaningful personal spiritual goals. Goals that will fortify your foundation and faith in Jesus Christ. Please remember to thank Him, He is the giver of all good gifts.

ELDER ULISSES SOARES

On one occasion, the Savior Himself said, "Therefore, what manner of men ought ye to be? Verily I say unto you, even as I am" (3 Nephi 27:27). This perfection certainly will not come until we reach the other side of the veil. Through His prophets, the Lord invites us to seek for ways to improve ourselves, never all at once, but line upon line.

The help we can receive from the Lord in our goals and righteous pursuits is unlimited, and He supports us in any good and righteous endeavor. My lifetime call as one of His special witnesses has added even more strength to my determination to continue to make improvements in various areas of my life in order to become more Christlike. Every effort to be more like Him increases our spiritual capacity to serve Him. We can always be grateful to the Lord for the help He gives us in making personal improvements. In my case, I still have a long way to go. But I'm making progress, little by little, with joy and gratitude!

I invite you to consider ways to pursue righteous endeavors in your own life, no matter your circumstances. I

> *He supports us in any good and righteous endeavor.*

assure you that the Lord loves each one of us and He is always there to help us, regardless of the situation we are facing.

PRESIDENT RUSSELL M. NELSON

For me, deep-sea fishing has been infrequent but instructive. Success requires patience, persistence, and prayer.

As we ... make resolutions to improve things in our lives, these three requisites for successful fishing can help us.

First, be patient. As with fishing, real change requires time—and often a lot of time. It is tempting to expect immediate results and then become disappointed when things don't work out exactly as planned. This may be why the Apostle Paul counseled us to "run with patience the race that is set before us" (Hebrews 12:1).

Second, be persistent. Keep at it, even when things get difficult. Push through the tough times, and realize that even small victories mean you are having success. The Savior "waxed strong in spirit" (Luke 2:40) as He grew older. We too can wax strong in spirit and in our talents and habits if we persevere.

Third, be prayerful. Call upon God for the strength you need as you labor diligently to become a better version of yourself—a better disciple of Jesus Christ, a brighter light in the world. For "they that wait upon the Lord shall renew their strength; they shall mount up with wings as eagles; they shall run, and not be weary; and they shall walk, and not faint" (Isaiah 40:31).

ELDER DALE G. RENLUND

Ruth and I decided we would . . . focus on our physical health. Together we have supported each other in making healthy food choices and getting plenty of exercise. We are now in better physical health. . . .

[Once], Ruth and I were hiking in one of the national parks in southern Utah. I realized that because of my attention to my health, the hike was much easier than the last time we were there—there was less of me to haul around, and it was exhilarating to feel stronger and healthier.

Getting rid of unhealthy debris—physical, mental, or emotional—in our lives is a powerful way to grow closer to our Savior. I testify that He is willing to help in all aspects of our lives. He wants to carry our burdens for us. He will carry our burdens and help us with the debris if we will but ask for His help and accept it when it comes.

> *Getting rid of unhealthy debris in our lives is a powerful way to grow closer to our Savior.*

ELDER DAVID A. BEDNAR

[The commandment to "be ye therefore perfect" (Matthew 5:48)] causes remarkable anxiety among the members of the Church, and it's a misinterpretation. In modern language, we think the word "perfect" means "perform without errors." That's not what it means in the scriptural context. It means "be therefore complete, as your Father in Heaven is complete." Here's how I think about *complete*. If you look at an apple tree in spring, it has blossoms, no apples. The blossom, if there's sunlight and water and other nutrients, turns it into a little, tiny bud. And the little, tiny apple, during the course of the spring and the summer, will continue to grow and mature. In the fall, it's now complete. And you pick the apple and have the delicious fruit. But who's the gardener? The Father and the Son. And we're connected by covenant. That's the source of the nutrients. What are we to become? Like them. Never in this life; never through our own works alone. Do we have to work at it? Absolutely. Is that enough? Never. And we stress out, thinking, "Oh, I'm never going to get it quite right." No, you're not. Neither am I. None of us are. But with His grace and with His help, incrementally and gradually, there's very steady growth just like the bud becomes an apple over time.

ELDER DIETER F. UCHTDORF

[My goal of becoming a professional pilot] was not easily achieved. In fact, when I chose to become a pilot, I also chose a long list of constraints.

To become the person I wanted to become, I knew that there would be many, many things I would have to do and an equally long list of things I would not allow myself to do.

I would have to go to school. I would have to approach my studies not with a casual attitude but with focus and concentration. I would need to give up hundreds of hours of

Work Toward Worthy Goals

entertainment for the work that would prepare me for the occupation I had chosen.

I invested, perhaps even sacrificed, a great deal to reach my goal. But I will tell you that the first time I climbed into the cockpit of a jet fighter and took it up into the air, I knew that my efforts—all the constraints I had chosen for myself—were well worth the effort.

> *As you choose to walk in the light, the influence of heaven will rest upon you.*

You, also, have the priceless blessing to choose who you wish to become. The very act of making choices of who you want to be requires setting aside other choices you might have made. But you do it willingly because the goal is greater than the sacrifice.

This is similar to what happens as we choose to become followers of Jesus Christ. We desire to become something more than who we currently are. We freely accept certain restrictions because it is necessary to do so in order to reach our higher and holier goals.

As you choose to walk in the light, the influence of heaven will rest upon you. The Spirit of God will support and guide you. His grace will attend you. You will discover how to seek and to follow the Savior's way in your life.

RELY ON THE
Holy Ghost

ELDER ULISSES SOARES

Just like a smartphone needs to be connected with a network to function properly, we need to connect with our Heavenly Father and Jesus Christ to receive guidance from heaven and spiritually survive in this complex world.

Our eternal progress depends on receiving personal guidance from the Holy Ghost. When we believe and trust that God wants to send us direction through the Holy Ghost, then, as we earnestly center our lives on pursuing heaven's help, we will receive the guidance we need according to the Lord's will and time.

PRESIDENT HENRY B. EYRING

I . . . had the privilege to confirm my eight-year-old granddaughter a member of The Church of Jesus Christ of Latter-day Saints. What an honor! As a holder of the

Melchizedek Priesthood, I also had the authority to place my hands on her head and say these words: "Receive the Holy Ghost." That was a command she had been prepared to receive as she had already taught us in a family devotional of the ... baptism of Jesus Christ and the appearance of the Holy Ghost in the form of a dove.

In her little lesson, she had used a soft baby blanket as her visual aid. She taught us that because of the Atonement of Jesus Christ, baptism can wash away sins and that we can feel the Holy Ghost's comfort and warmth, just like the blanket.

There are so many ways to hear Him.

Even a little child can feel the comforting voice of the Spirit. She, and all of us, can take heart as our faith in Jesus Christ grows and we continually increase our capacity to have the Holy Ghost as a constant companion.

My testimony is that the Holy Ghost is a personage of Spirit. I have felt His comfort and direction countless times in my life. It helps me to know that the companionship of the Holy Ghost is a gift, not only a reward for our efforts. I promise you that your fervent prayers—in the name of Jesus Christ—to receive the blessings and fruits of Holy Ghost, even the still small voice, can and will be answered.

Rely on the Holy Ghost

ELDER DIETER F. UCHTDORF

There are so many ways to hear Him. My most personal experiences—when I think of the Savior, how He loves me, and then how much I love Him—this is for me like a bridge or a connection or a door which opens. Because then I feel the power and the gift of the Holy Ghost. It is that love which is the key, I think. When I'm not grateful, I cannot feel this love. And when I'm grateful for the Savior and for what the Lord has given me, then this love opens doors and opens a stream of things which I have heard or seen or done before, which will help me to make the right decisions. I've seen this in my professional life, that at moments where I didn't know what to do and I could find a quiet spot and connect to Heavenly Father and to His Son, Jesus Christ, by the gift of the Holy Ghost, over the bridge of love to Them, then all of a sudden, this stream of answers came to me. This is how He speaks to me, and it is when I'm focusing on the love He has for us and my love for Him. This carries me on to answers and responses which I'm so in need of now, and I've been in need of throughout my life.

Trust
IN GOD

ELDER NEIL L. ANDERSEN

Climbing the mountain of mortality can be very hard; but eternity can be absolutely exhilarating, and the view then, spectacular—beyond our grandest imagination.

So hold on to the commandments of God and your sacred covenants and keep climbing. And if you need to sit down for a moment or a time, if you only have strength for this hour or this day, then rest and go to your knees—physically or in your mind—and pray to your Heavenly Father.

Even if your ascension is an inch at a time, you will make it.

Angels have been promised to bear you up.

They will.

You can and you will make it.

Never give up.

Keep climbing, even if your ascension is an inch at a time, you will make it. God loves you.

ELDER DALE G. RENLUND

The infuriating unfairness that abounds in this fallen world causes many to reject God's existence. I can understand why some might come to that conclusion, but I declare and believe with all my heart that, because of His great atoning sacrifice, the Savior, Jesus Christ, recognizes and understands unfairness and will ultimately compensate for any unfairness inflicted on you or on any of Heavenly Father's children.

However, you and I may want to know, "How? How is Jesus Christ going to do that?" To my knowledge, God has not revealed "how" to His prophets, seers, and revelators. What I do know is that for us to insist on knowing "how" before we begin to trust in and develop faith in Him and His promises is misguided. It ignores the reality of what God did reveal to Isaiah about Himself: "For my thoughts are not your thoughts, neither are your ways my ways, saith the Lord" (Isaiah 55:8).

Hold your questions about "how" for later and work on developing faith in Heavenly Father and His plan and in Jesus Christ and His Atonement. Work to "believe in God; believe that he is, and that he created all things, both in heaven and in earth; believe that he has all wisdom, and all power, both in heaven and in earth; believe that man doth not comprehend all the things which the Lord can comprehend" (Mosiah 4:9).

ELDER GERRIT W. GONG

We sometimes wait upon the Lord. We may not yet be where we hope or wish to be in the future.

Isaiah's promise is real: "They that wait upon the Lord shall renew their strength; they shall mount up with wings as eagles; they shall run, and not be weary; and they shall walk, and not faint" (Isaiah 40:31).

Trust God. He knows us better and loves us more than we know or love ourselves. His love and knowledge are infinite and perfect. His covenants and promises are constant and sure.

PRESIDENT JEFFREY R. HOLLAND

Wherever I go—and wherever you are—we find people who've had disappointments. We find people who've had heartache. We see things that are broken in our life. It's a little bit like having your great-grandmother's precious piece of china saved on the trip over from England two centuries ago. And suddenly you have an accident in the home, and that little piece of china is broken. Almost it would appear to be irreparable. You couldn't get it back. Well, in the gospel of Jesus Christ, you get it back. And things are broken regularly.

It takes broken clouds to nourish the earth. It takes broken earth to grow grain. It takes broken grain to make bread. It takes broken bread to feed us. These are the cycles of life.

> *His covenants and promises are constant and sure.*

Like that parable that the Savior taught where he said, "Unless a man cast away his kernel of corn"— corn being the translation for wheat—unless he cast it away in the spring, he won't have that harvest in the fall [see John 12:24]. And that's the way it is with us. We have to manage this and live with it. And when there's a broken dream or a broken marriage, broken unity with the children in the family? Well, there's an answer to that. We can survive that. It's going to grow if we live the gospel. Plant that seed. It's going to come back to us at harvest time, rich and abundant, and it'll be better than it was before.

Trust in God

One of the reasons that it works is because we offer a sacrifice that's also broken, and ours is a broken heart and a contrite spirit. If we will be that humble, . . . if we can be more humble, if we can be more like a child, if we can be more receptive to the Spirit of the Lord, we're going to be healed too. We're going to be put back together. Marriages will, and families will, and financial challenges will. They'll all be improved, finally, to perfection. And that's what the gospel of Jesus Christ offers. Through the Savior's Atonement, through His sacrifice for us, our sacrifices, little as they are, our sacrifices then take on real meaning, and a broken heart is given back to us. And we have the stature and the dignity and the faith and the purpose of someone who's better than they knew they were, better than they thought things could be. And that all comes from a little parable about throwing away a kernel of corn. And we reap the benefit of a saving, loving, atoning Jesus Christ, who accepts our gift and gives it back. And we're renewed. We're born again. We're whole and complete and powerful as long as we live that gospel principle that brought us there.

God will help us *Through* our trials

ELDER ULISSES SOARES

We should remember that although we face difficult trials, they are part of our mortal experience. Remember that our mortal life is temporary, and our individual trials are designed to test our faith to see if we will do what the Lord asked us to do before we came to earth.

I have gone through many trials in my own life—some of those challenges involved the loss of loved ones or health issues. In those trials, I found that I was closer to my Heavenly Father. I promise you that if you will press forward, strengthening your faith, and show your Heavenly Father that you are faithful, you will receive divine help. Heavenly Father wants nothing more than to bring us back to His presence. I testify that He is eager to hear your prayers and help you through your trials.

He is eager to hear your prayers and help you through your trials.

DIRECT MESSAGES

PRESIDENT HENRY B. EYRING

Our mortal life is designed by a loving God to be a test and source of growth for each of us.

Since the beginning, the tests have not been easy. We face trials that come from having mortal bodies. All of us live in a world where Satan's war against truth and against our personal happiness is becoming more intense. The world and your life can seem to you to be in increasing commotion.

My reassurance is this: the loving God who allowed these tests for you also designed a sure way to pass through them. Heavenly Father so loved the world that He sent His Beloved Son to help us [see John 3:16]. His Son, Jesus Christ, gave His life for us. Jesus Christ bore in Gethsemane and on the cross the weight of all our sins. He experienced all the sorrows, the pains, and the effects of our sins so that He could comfort and strengthen us through every test in life.

I bear you my witness that the Savior knows and loves you. He knows your name as you know His. He knows your troubles. He has experienced them. By His Atonement, He has overcome the world.

God Will Help Us Through Our Trials

ELDER QUENTIN L. COOK

The world is full of raging conflicts, burning contentions, and heavy burdens. These difficult circumstances can threaten our homes and weaken our spirits.

However, despite these challenging times, there is always hope.

As we rely on Jesus Christ and His Atonement, He will help us endure trials, sickness, and pain. He will fill us with joy, peace, and consolation.

All that is unfair about life can be made right through the Atonement of Jesus Christ.

ELDER GERRIT W. GONG

When we are doing the best we can—we're living the gospel, we're serving in the Church—sometimes, still, bad things can happen to good people....

He says, "I will wipe away the tears, all the tears, except the tears of joy" [see Isaiah 25:8–9]. My testimony is when we weep, He also weeps. When bad things happen to His children, I think He may be closer to us then than we may ever know.

ELDER RONALD A. RASBAND

Life has always been filled with challenges. No one is immune. Several years ago, our grandson Paxton was born with an extremely rare genetic disorder. He struggled mightily with his health until he passed away after only three short years here on earth.

> *When you take steps toward Him, He will come to you.*

Watching Paxton struggle and ultimately pass away was one of the most heart-wrenching experiences of my life. We ached for him to receive relief from his grueling challenges. Yet, thanks to our understanding of the gospel of Jesus Christ, we also knew that he was known and loved by our Heavenly Father.

Problems, challenges, trials, tribulations, hardships, miseries—call them what you will—are part of this mortal experience to make us strong and build us up. While we still dearly miss our grandson, we are lifted by the awe-inspiring

God Will Help Us Through Our Trials

message that through the Atonement of Jesus Christ we can find hope in trials and be of good cheer.

To be of good cheer is to trust Him when things don't work as planned. It means to carry on when difficult twists in life take us in unexpected directions or when tragedy and hardship shatter our ideals.

Christ's enabling power is manifest in the simplicity that He is there for us—always. Come what may, He will be with us, He will comfort us, and He will heal us if we come to Him and draw upon His power to save us.

We will see our grandson again. And he will be healthy and strong, thanks to the atoning sacrifice of Jesus Christ and our Father's perfect plan.

PRESIDENT JEFFREY R. HOLLAND

Life is a gift—but it also has difficulties. On this journey of life, you will face times of hardship, personal trial, discouragement, and disappointment that can feel overwhelming. Perhaps you feel trapped in such a time right now.

During such times, please remember that your Heavenly Father loves you. He always has, and He always will. Because of His infinite and perfect love, He sent His Son, Jesus Christ, to strengthen you and help you move forward. And Jesus came because He loves you deeply too.

With all my heart, I testify that Jesus is the Christ. When you take steps toward Him, reach for Him, and invite Him to be your strength, He will come to you and you will find Him. There is no choice you can make that somehow places you beyond His reach.

BE A
Peacemaker

PRESIDENT RUSSELL M. NELSON

Differences of opinion are part of life. I work daily with people who sometimes see an issue differently. My two noble counselors, Dallin H. Oaks and Henry B. Eyring, have taught me how to disagree in a Christlike way. [While] working together, we haven't always agreed. Still, they know I want to hear their honest feelings about everything we discuss—especially sensitive issues.

From their examples, I have learned six ways to disagree:

Express feelings with love.

Don't think you know best.

Don't compete.

Don't rigorously defend your position.

Let the Spirit guide your conversations.

Be filled with charity, the pure love of Christ.

Charity is the antidote to contention. It is the principal

characteristic of a true follower of Jesus Christ. Charity defines a peacemaker.

PRESIDENT HENRY B. EYRING

"Blessed are the peacemakers" [Matthew 5:9].

I testify to you that I know the Savior spoke truth when He said this. I pray that each of you will offer peace, and so as peacemakers become the children of God.

You may well doubt that you can have much effect on the people around you. When you act with faith to offer the gospel and peace to those around you, the light that will come to them will be more than your example and more than your words. They will feel the light of the Savior, and it will have drawn them to Him.

ELDER NEIL L. ANDERSEN

As followers of Jesus Christ, we must genuinely love and care for all of God's children—just as He does—without isolating ourselves from others who believe differently.

Be a Peacemaker

Jesus lovingly washed the feet of His Apostles, knowing what would occur soon after. Although "he was troubled in spirit" (John 13:21) as He thought about one He loved preparing to betray Him, Jesus interestingly spoke no more about His "troubled" feelings, instead choosing to speak to His Apostles about love:

"A new commandment I give unto you, That ye love one another; as I have loved you. . . .

"By this shall all men know that ye are my disciples, if ye have love one to another" (John 13:34–35).

Whether it be a friend with different religious beliefs, a neighbor with conflicting political views, a relative experiencing a faith crisis, or a colleague making lifestyle choices opposite of what you would choose, all people on earth are "the offspring of God" (Acts 17:29) and are loved by Him.

Let us reconcile our differences and become peacemakers, as our Savior Jesus Christ invites us.

ELDER DIETER F. UCHTDORF

As fellow sons and daughters of our Heavenly Father, we have the responsibility and opportunity to promote peace and harmony among all of God's children. . . .

DIRECT MESSAGES

I have shared before that if we only would focus on the life experiences and hopes we have in common, it should not be too hard to get along with individuals, communities, and nations—regardless of where we live and regardless of what our backgrounds or life circumstances may be.

> *We must genuinely love and care for all of God's children.*

If world history has taught us anything, we learn that it is a human tendency to think of ourselves as being the "good guys"—as the heroes of the story. And those who think and behave differently? Well, they are the "bad guys." When we see others as enemies, we look for the worst in them and the best in us.

The gospel of Jesus Christ teaches us to magnify the love in our heart until we see all men and women as our neighbors—as our brothers and sisters. His gospel unites and unifies every man, woman, and child. It teaches that we are not enemies but are of one divine and eternal family: sons and daughters of a loving Heavenly Father.

THE LORD *Restored* THE *Gospel* THROUGH JOSEPH SMITH

PRESIDENT DALLIN H. OAKS

In all of my reading and original research about Joseph Smith, I have never been dissuaded from my testimony of his prophetic calling and of the gospel and priesthood restoration the Lord initiated through him.

ELDER GARY E. STEVENSON

Joseph Smith was seventeen when Moroni revealed to him an ancient record, another testament of Jesus Christ, engraved on plates.... Joseph was tutored by this heavenly messenger annually for four years, when finally given stewardship of the plates at age twenty-one ... for the translation and publication as the Book of Mormon. The testimony of eight witnesses who also saw the plates and of three witnesses—Martin Harris, Oliver Cowdery, and David Whitmer—who saw and held the plates in the presence of an angel, give insight into the construction and physical characteristics of the plates.... But more importantly, they give us a testimony of the truthfulness of the Book of Mormon as the word of God. Perhaps the greatest witness of the truthfulness of the Book of Mormon comes from the Lord Jesus Christ Himself, when in revelation, referring to the work of the Prophet Joseph Smith, proclaims, "And he has translated the book, even that part which I have commanded him, and as your Lord and your God liveth it is true" [Doctrine and Covenants 17:6]. May I ... add my testimony of this marvelous heavenly visitation and that the Book of Mormon is the word of God.

ELDER DALE G. RENLUND

I am grateful for all [Joseph Smith] did to establish the Church of Christ on the earth. Not only was he intimately involved in the restoration of doctrinal truths to the earth; he also advocated for the rights of the Saints to exercise their religious beliefs.

He petitioned governments, met with the president of the United States, and was repeatedly jailed because of his faith. Before the presidential election in 1844, he wrote to the five candidates for president to see if any of them would help the Saints recover their properties in Missouri. None would help.

> *Joseph Smith gave his all for the Lord and His Church.*

With encouragement of the leaders of the Church, Joseph Smith declared his candidacy for president. His platform included constitutional reform, prison reform, banking reform, and the abolition of slavery. He was forward-thinking and advocated for the human dignity of all God's children and their rights of self-determination. He was the first US presidential candidate to be assassinated.

I admire and love Joseph Smith, who gave his all for the Lord and His Church. His assassination proved the point of his running for president: that religious freedom and self-determination needed to be protected for all.

ELDER DAVID A. BEDNAR

One of the questions that I frequently am asked is, "What does it mean that the restoration is ongoing?" Let me answer that question with an article of faith and two scriptures. First is the ninth article of faith: "We believe all that God has revealed, all that he does now reveal, and we believe that he will yet reveal many great and important things pertaining to the Kingdom of God." What He will yet reveal alludes to the ongoing nature of the restoration.

Second is in the twenty-first section of the Doctrine and Covenants. This is specifically to the Prophet Joseph Smith, beginning in verse 1: "Behold, there shall be a record kept among you; and in it thou shalt be called a seer, a translator, a prophet, an apostle of Jesus Christ, an elder of the church, through the will of God the Father, and the grace of your Lord Jesus Christ." Now please note this: "Being inspired of the Holy Ghost to lay the foundation thereof, and to build it up unto the most holy faith. Which church was organized and established in the year of your Lord [1830]" [vv. 2–3].

> *Joseph Smith received what was necessary to lay the foundation of the Church.*

Joseph Smith didn't receive everything. He received what was necessary to lay the foundation of the Church. So if you've watched a home being built, you put in the foundation, you put up the exterior walls, and it takes a long time for all the finishing work to be accomplished to finally have a finished home. Joseph specifically was described as laying the foundation. So all of that additional construction, if you will, is the ongoing nature of the Restoration.

Third verse is the 128th section of the Doctrine and Covenants: "For it is necessary in the ushering in of the dispensation of the fulness of times, which dispensation is now beginning to usher in, that a whole and complete and perfect union, and welding together of dispensations, and keys, and powers, and glories should take place, and be revealed from the days of Adam even to the present time. And not only this, but those things which never have been revealed from the foundation of the world, but have been kept hid from the wise and prudent, shall be revealed ... [in] the dispensation of the fulness of times" [v. 18]. So just to summarize, Joseph didn't receive everything. He received all that was necessary to establish the foundation. And we believe all that God has revealed, and all that He will yet reveal. That is the ongoing nature of the Restoration.

Minister AND *Serve* LIKE CHRIST

ELDER DIETER F. UCHTDORF

The Savior's teachings about our relationship with our Heavenly Father and with one another are straightforward: Love God and serve Him, then love our neighbors and serve them.

Don't make it too complicated. We have received a responsibility to love all of God's children and invite all to come and see—to learn more about the restored gospel of Jesus Christ. Invite them to our sacrament meeting. Keep it simple. We love, share, and invite.

ELDER ULISSES SOARES

Jesus Christ is our perfect example of charity. We seek to follow His example as we minister to those in need....

As we pursue and develop the attribute of charity, we will become more sensitive to the needs of our fellow beings. We will experience joy, peace, and spiritual growth.

Our efforts will make us as individuals and society a better place.

ELDER QUENTIN L. COOK

A story is told of an English cathedral that was bombed during the Second World War. By the end of the war, many repairs had to be made to the cathedral.

There was also a beautiful statue of the Savior, and one of the bombs had blown away the statue's hands. Initially, they decided to have the statue repaired, but after consideration decided instead to put a sign next to the handless statue that read, "Christ has no hands but yours."

In the Doctrine and Covenants, the Savior uses these words: "Yea, I will open the hearts of the people. . . . And I will establish a church by your hand" (Doctrine and Covenants 31:7).

> *Keep it simple. We love, share, and invite.*

The principal way we can show our gratitude to the Savior for what He has done for us is to be His servants—to, in effect, be His hands here on earth.

Our love of God and our fellowmen is the ultimate test of the condition of our spirit. If we love God, we will keep

His commandments. And if we love our fellowmen, we will serve them.

> ### ELDER GARY E. STEVENSON
>
> Friends, ministering is the higher and holier way to love those around us. As we minister, we help fulfill the two great commandments: to love God with all our hearts and love our neighbors as we love ourselves. The Savior is our perfect example. He ministered to those around Him regardless of the inconvenience of time or circumstance. We are living in trying times and unusual circumstances, and so many of us desperately need to feel His love.
>
> I invite you to find opportunities . . . to follow our Savior's example and find ways to minister with love to those around you.

ELDER GERRIT W. GONG

The Lord gives us divine opportunity to become more like Him as we offer proxy saving temple ordinances others need but cannot do for themselves. We become more complete and perfected as we become "saviours . . . on mount Zion," as it says in Obadiah 1:21. As we serve others, the Holy Spirit of Promise can ratify the ordinances and sanctify both giver and receiver. Both giver and receiver can make and deepen transforming covenants, over time, receiving the blessings promised Abraham, Isaac, and Jacob.

ELDER DIETER F. UCHTDORF

You may experience moments when you wonder what you can do to make an impact on the world. Early on, I learned that if you want to change the world, you need to first change yourself.

I love the experience of Gordon B. Hinckley as a young missionary when his father told him, "Forget about yourself and go to work." The world needs your enthusiasm, your energy, your faith, your testimony. There are many ways you can share your light and make the world a better place.

Recently I was impressed by the experiences of two of my grandchildren—Robin and Jasmin. They volunteered as For the Strength of Youth conference counselors. They worked and served with young people who have common goals, questions, and challenges. They had fun experiences.

They greatly enjoyed it. Another of my grandsons is now applying to be a counselor this year. . . .

No matter how you choose to share the light you have, others will benefit from your experiences. You will draw closer to the Savior when you engage in wholesome activities and serve others. I promise it will change you and the world for the better.

PRESIDENT RUSSELL M. NELSON

What does the word "love" really mean? Is it about flowers, chocolate, and gifts? Certainly, at times, it can be. But the second great commandment teaches of a different kind of love—that of actively loving our neighbor.

Giving help to others—making a conscientious effort to care about others as much as or more than we care about ourselves—is our joy. Especially, I might add, when it is not convenient and when it takes us out of our comfort zone. Living that second great commandment is the key to becoming a true disciple of Jesus Christ.

Find ways to minister with love to those around you.

Of course, we must remember that the second great

commandment follows an even greater commandment—which is the commandment to first love God.

We often see people in the world today ignore the first commandment. And yet, when we obey the first commandment, we are much better equipped to keep the second commandment.

> *Living that second great commandment is the key to becoming a true disciple of Jesus Christ.*

It has been my privilege to witness the impact of many humanitarian efforts around the world made by The Church of Jesus Christ of Latter-day Saints. . . . May we . . . recommit to loving our neighbor—whether they live in the house next door or across the globe.

PRESIDENT RUSSELL M. NELSON

I invite you to consider prayerfully: Who do you know who may be discouraged? Who might you need to reconcile with or ask for forgiveness? Has one name been on your mind lately, though you haven't quite known why? As you bring these questions to the Lord, He will inspire you to know how you can reach out and lift one who needs help.

Minister and Serve Like Christ

What a beautiful example the Savior has shown us—that through each of us ministering to just one within our reach, we can spread the love of Jesus Christ throughout the world.

Teach the *Gospel* in the savior's *Way*

ELDER DAVID A. BEDNAR

As we teach, testify, answer questions, and help friends to learn for themselves, we have a sacred responsibility to maintain the purity of gospel doctrine and principles. All of us should avoid speculating about subjects on which little or nothing has been revealed, perpetuating unsubstantiated claims and rumors, and substituting personal opinions and experiences for the word of God. We individually should pay the price to learn and understand the doctrine and principles for ourselves by the power of the Holy Ghost: We must own it!

ELDER QUENTIN L. COOK

Preach My Gospel emphasizes the inclusive nature of the gospel of Jesus Christ. God invites "all to come unto him and partake of his goodness; and he denieth none that come unto him" (2 Nephi 26:33). This is true regardless of race or culture.

Regardless of our family situations on earth, each of us is a member of the family of God. Both individuals and families are most likely to be happy when living by the teachings of Jesus Christ. And as we are faithful, God will provide a way for us to have the blessings of loving families, whether in this life or the life to come.

Through ordinances and covenants, families can be united for eternity. Helping individuals and families receive the blessings of eternal life is central to the missionary purpose.

I invite you to study and learn from *Preach My Gospel*. The principles it teaches can help each of us share the Savior's gospel and invite others to come unto Him. This sacred responsibility is not just for a select few but for all who have made covenants with God and seek to follow His Son.

ELDER NEIL L. ANDERSEN

I [would like to share] five principles that are important for missionaries in The Church of Jesus Christ of

Latter-day Saints to understand as they invite people to make and keep commitments.

Additionally, these principles are important for all of us to understand as we do our part to invite people to follow Jesus Christ and as we strengthen our own foundations of faith:

1. Making and keeping commitments lead the honest in heart to making and keeping sacred covenants with God.
2. Inviting someone to make a commitment is often an invitation to repent.
3. Acting in faith to better follow Jesus Christ brings His love and the truth of His teachings.
4. Spiritual power comes from exercising one's own will and agency—no compulsion, no manipulation.
5. The timing and tone of invitations are individually shaped and inspired.

Invitations will be more readily accepted as those we teach know why accepting the invitation will move them forward in their spiritual journey. Our Savior, Jesus Christ, is the way, the truth, and the life. All eternal happiness comes from Him.

PRESIDENT RUSSELL M. NELSON

The Lord declared two millennia ago, "Go ye therefore, and teach all nations, baptizing them in the name of the Father, and of the Son, and of the Holy Ghost" (Matthew 28:19). That commandment is still in force, made vital again by the Savior's coming to the earth, under the direction of God the Father, to the Prophet Joseph Smith to restore the gospel of Jesus Christ in its fulness and to reestablish His Church. As members of the Church, we have the sacred and covenant responsibility to share the gospel of Jesus Christ and bless the lives of all of God's children.

ELDER RONALD A. RASBAND

A large part of missionary work includes sharing the Book of Mormon with others. When I think of this, I recall a specific experience of one of our missionaries when I served as a mission president.

During his final testimony on his mission, he shared

Teach the Gospel in the Savior's Way

that he loved his mission but expressed his disappointment about serving in one specific area in this manner: "All I did there was pass out copies of the Book of Mormon on a street corner." I will never forget his admission of disappointment and his feeling that his effort was wasted.

But the story doesn't end there. Months later, another missionary shared that the highlight of his mission was teaching a single mother of four. This woman was completely overwhelmed with the challenges of life and decided to pray for God's help. When she looked up from her prayer, she saw the

> *What we do might not bring immediate results, but they may have unseen, lasting impacts.*

Book of Mormon on her shelf. She opened the book and began to read. On the back cover was a stamp with a missionary phone number. She called that number, was taught the precious truths of the gospel, and was soon baptized.

You might have guessed it by now, but this copy of the Book of Mormon was one of the copies shared by the other missionary on a street corner just a few months earlier—a missionary who felt discouraged because he didn't see the results he had hoped for from his efforts.

As those who share the gospel of Jesus Christ, we don't always see the future consequences of our efforts to share the gospel. What we do might not bring immediate results, but they may have unseen, lasting impacts.

ELDER DAVID A. BEDNAR

As we focus on the work of proclaiming the gospel, we emphasize "just be normal and natural." If an individual or a family would consider just their normal, natural routine, what's something that they would be interested in posting and just sharing? It doesn't have to be a gospel message. We *are* the gospel message. I think it could help people to understand that what we do is much more important than what we may write or say.

So some of the very normal things that we do—it may be that someone would simply highlight one aspect of a family home evening, and it might be that a young child would be giving a lesson. Now, *we* all think that's normal, but that's abnormal, in a home, to have a child taking the lead in providing some instruction. Well, [share] a few segments about that. A little commentary about "Here's what we focused on. We were talking about prayer because in our home, we believe prayer is important," and then have the little kid [answer the question,] "What was it like for you to give this lesson?" People would just be blown away to think that a six- or seven-year-old kid could give a lesson.

So it's just so normal, natural, small increments, line upon line. That's how you get started. You gain a little experience. You see what works, what doesn't work. That's what we do. There are things that we say, "Let's try this. Well, that didn't work very well, so?" But you learn something about what your next episode will be. So, I would just invite people to be prayerful. Consider the normal, natural flow of your life, and what can you do about your life, about your family, about your children, that highlights the gospel. But it's not an in-your-face, overt, "come have the missionaries come to your home." Just live the gospel. Let some of that be in your social media posts, and it will create a curiosity. We live a distinctive lifestyle, and if we just have natural elements of that lifestyle, some folks are going to find that pretty interesting. I think the light that will be associated with the messages that come from authentic disciples of the Lord Jesus Christ will become ever more attractive. In a world where people will use these tools to enhance the darkness, the light will shine ever brighter.

DIRECT MESSAGES

ELDER D. TODD CHRISTOFFERSON

As missionaries and as disciples of Jesus Christ, we desire to bring more people to the Savior. To do that, we must help others understand the Book of Mormon: Another Testament of Jesus Christ. As [we] teach about the Book of Mormon, [we] should consider the following:

> *We desire to bring more people to the Savior.*

- Pray before reading. Ask for help in understanding. Pray that the Holy Ghost will witness to those searching for truth that the words in the Book of Mormon are true.
- Take turns reading. Go at a pace those who are studying are comfortable with. Explain unfamiliar words and phrases.
- Stop occasionally to discuss what you read.
- Explain the background and context of the passage, such as who is speaking, what the person is like, and what the situation is.
- Share your testimony and appropriate insights, feelings, and personal experiences.

Remember that in all of this, you are trying to help

people learn how to read the Book of Mormon on their own. You want to help them develop a desire to read the Book of Mormon daily. Reading and studying the Book of Mormon each day, even if at times it is only a few verses, is key to our own lifelong conversion.

THE SAVIOR *Promises* US *Peace*

PRESIDENT HENRY B. EYRING

The Savior has promised each of us peace in this life. At times, you may long for peace as you face uncertainty and what seem to you to be looming challenges.

Because of the Atonement of Jesus Christ, the constant companionship of the Holy Ghost will have a sanctifying and purifying effect on your spirit. You will then feel the peace the Savior promised to leave with you.

With that peace will come a bright hope and a feeling of light and love from the Father and His Beloved Son, who leads His kingdom on earth through revelation to His living prophet.

ELDER GERRIT W. GONG

The scriptures tell us that in the last days, "all things shall be in commotion" (Doctrine and Covenants 88:91). The scriptures were written for our time, and they reflect

> *Our living Savior Jesus Christ calls to each of us individually.*

our challenges. We certainly see commotion and uncertainty around us today.

But the scriptures also give us a promise of peace. We learn in the Book of Mormon that our Savior, Jesus Christ, suffered "pains and afflictions and temptations of every kind," so that He could "succor his people according to their infirmities" (Alma 7:11–12).

I am grateful for the inspiration, guidance, peace, and pattern of revelation we find in the scriptures. The Lord comforts and inspires me as I immerse myself in the scriptures, and I know He will also comfort and inspire you. He encircles us eternally "in the arms of his love" (2 Nephi 1:15).

ELDER RONALD A. RASBAND

Just as He appeared to Mary Magdalene at the garden tomb—calling her by name (see John 20:16)—our living Savior Jesus Christ calls to each of us individually, inviting us to turn to Him.

In the New Testament we read, "Mary stood without at the sepulchre weeping" (John 20:11). In our lives, there may be times we weep in hope for a miracle to heal a loved one, to reverse an unjust act, or to soften the heart of a bitter or disillusioned soul.

But the Lord has reminded us, "For my thoughts are not your thoughts, neither are your ways my ways" (Isaiah 55:8). He offers, "Come unto me, all ye that labour and are heavy laden, and I will give you rest" (Matthew 11:28)—rest from worry, disappointment, fear, disobedience, concern for loved ones, for lost or broken dreams.

Peace amid confusion or sorrow is a miracle. Jesus offers this promise to each of us, the same as He did for Mary that Resurrection Day.

PRESIDENT HENRY B. EYRING

One of the most beautiful symbols of the birth of Jesus Christ into this world is light. The appearance of the long-promised Messiah brought light to a darkened world.

Many of you are praying for the strength to endure trials that test you to what may feel to you like your limit. God knows our every need, He loves us, and He watches over us. He gave us the gift of a Savior, His perfect Son. He is the Light of the World and the sure source of comfort, hope, peace, and joy.

Elevate YOUR

PERSPECTIVE

ELDER GARY E. STEVENSON

Our outlook on life can change as we expand our gospel vision and elevate our spiritual vantage point. The Spirit can teach us what we need to change to give our lives balance and prepare us to embrace the future with faith.

PRESIDENT JEFFREY R. HOLLAND

Dream dreams. Dream dreams and see visions. You know the verse I'm talking about? [See Joel 2:28]. One of the verses that Moroni told Joseph Smith, which he came to tell him four times. He repeats to him that verse from Joel. I think that means—from Moroni to Joseph—"Joseph, you better dream dreams and see more visions, because that's where this church is going."

> *Embrace the future with faith.*

. . . We have to be among that group that dreams dreams and sees visions. Whatever you think the Church is going to be, it's going to be a lot more than that. It is the one thing that I know for sure is going to succeed. I'm not sure about economies. I'm not sure about politics. I'm not sure about businesses. I'm not sure about universities or hospitals. I don't know what's going to work and what's going to fail. But I know one thing that's going to work. And I know one thing that is never, ever, ever going to fail. And it is the restored gospel of Jesus Christ. It is this Church, your priesthood, and our destiny. So take the blinders off. "Think outside the box," we say these days. Don't just do it because we've always done it. Dream dreams and see visions. Thank you for participating in the greatest miracle going forth on this earth, the final dispensation. No more after this. It's going to be over when this is over. And so, we're supposed to dream our way to the finish, all the way to the end.

ELDER DAVID A. BEDNAR

Binoculars are optical instruments designed for simultaneous use by both eyes to help us to see distant things more clearly. Like telescopes, binoculars magnify objects and make them easier to see. But a person uses only one eye to look through a telescope. Both eyes are used to look through binoculars, thus making objects look more realistic.

Just as our vision of something far distant is sharpened by using both eyes with a pair of binoculars, so too our eternal purpose and priorities are clarified as we appropriately strive to balance and apply in our lives the dual principles of "believing to see" and "seeing to believe."

The Lord emphasizes this vital balance in His admonition for us to "seek learning even by study and also by faith" (Doctrine and Covenants 109:7).

> *Obtain eyes of faith to receive and recognize direction that comes from God.*

You and I have a spiritual responsibility to exercise our moral agency and, to the best of our ability, think and work and study out in our own minds an issue or problem. But we expend this effort in preparation to sincerely and humbly seek God's confirmation of our proposal.

Rather than rely only upon our own intellect and capacity, we strive to obtain eyes of faith to receive and recognize direction that comes from God by the power of the

Holy Ghost. Truly, believing is seeing what we otherwise could never see and learning what we otherwise could never learn.

Each of us should be wise and not be seduced to rely exclusively on the principle of "seeing is believing." Doing so will restrict and constrain our understanding of the things that truly matter the most in our lives.

ELDER DIETER F. UCHTDORF

Most of you are feeling your way through the obstacles of daily life and trying to find your place in the world. Like for any of us, getting through each day is a challenge. You even might have physical, emotional, or spiritual challenges that press upon you almost every day. [Airplanes] have the capacity of defying gravity, climbing higher and higher and soaring onto new horizons. How I wanted to sit in the cockpit of one of those beautiful flying machines. I knew that the fulfillment of such a dream would not come easily. Because my dream was so compelling, these things stopped being obligations. Instead, they became opportunities. Yes, they were difficult. Yes, at times the effort seemed too hard, and I wanted to quit. But I knew if I pressed on, if I gave it my all, the Lord would help me, for with God, nothing is impossible. I want you also to know that you are not alone. Your Heavenly Father knows you. He hears your prayers. He is aware of your every tear. He loves you with infinite love and watches over you. Even when you might feel you are alone, you are not because He is always there.

Priesthood AUTHORITY Blesses GOD'S CHILDREN

ELDER DAVID A. BEDNAR

Among the] miraculous experiences [in the organization of the Church] was the restoration of the priesthood authority that was lost from the earth. This authority allows God's servants to represent Him and act in His name. Under the direction of the Father and the Son, the resurrected John the Baptist restored the authority to baptize by immersion for the remission of sins in 1829. In that same year, three of the original twelve Apostles—Peter, James, and John— restored the apostleship and additional priesthood authority and keys. Priesthood keys are the authority to direct the use of the priesthood on behalf of God's children, and a fundamental component in formally organizing the Savior's restored Church.

I joyfully witness that the Father and the Son appeared to the boy Joseph Smith, thus initiating the Restoration of the gospel of Jesus Christ in the latter days. The Book of Mormon is another testament of Jesus Christ and contains the word of God. Priesthood authority to represent the Savior, and act in His name, again is found on the earth, and The Church of Jesus Christ of Latter-day Saints is Christ's New Testament Church restored.

ELDER NEIL L. ANDERSEN

What a blessing to have the priesthood in our families! What a blessing to have the temple for our grandchildren! ...

Performing temple work and living up to sacred priesthood duties will unite families on both sides of the veil. ... In the temple, we feel power from on high to face challenges in our personal lives and within our families. Our love for one another and for the Savior grows as we focus on the eternal nature of our relationships.

PRESIDENT DALLIN H. OAKS

The idea that a person can be spiritual or worship God without organized religion is popular in our day. Some may wonder, "Why do we need a church?"

Priesthood Authority Blesses God's Children

While developing a relationship with God is personal and can certainly progress independent of church participation, The Church of Jesus Christ of Latter-day Saints exists to teach the fulness of His doctrine and officiate with His priesthood authority to perform the ordinances necessary to enter the kingdom of God with our loved ones forever.

In other words, church attendance and participation help us focus on our eternal priorities. In addition, those who forgo church attendance and rely only on individual spirituality forfeit many opportunities to make sacred covenants with God, including in holy temples, or qualify to perpetuate their family for eternity.

> *Priesthood authority to represent the Savior is found on the earth,*

The Bible teaches that Jesus Christ is "the head of the church" (Ephesians 5:23) and that He organized it "for the perfecting of the saints, for the work of the ministry, for the edifying of the body of Christ" (Ephesians 4:12). We affirm the scriptural origin and need for a church directed by and with the authority of our Lord, Jesus Christ.

Prepare for the *Savior's* Return

ELDER QUENTIN L. COOK

As we contemplate our spiritual condition and our preparation to greet the Savior, we should first "love the Lord thy God with all thy heart, and with all thy soul, and with all thy mind" (Matthew 22:37).

And second, "love thy neighbour as thyself" (Matthew 22:39).

Our love of God and our fellow man is the ultimate test of the condition of our spirit. If we love God, we will keep His commandments. And if we love our fellow men, we will serve them and essentially be the Savior's hands.

PRESIDENT DALLIN H. OAKS

People often inquire about the exact time of the Second Coming.

While we cannot know that (see Matthew 24:36), what if the day of His coming were tomorrow? If you knew that

> *He shall come, as He has promised.*

you would meet the Lord tomorrow—through premature death or through His unexpected coming—what would you do today?

As Jesus taught in His prophecy of the Second Coming, blessed is the "faithful and wise servant" who is attending to his duty when the Lord comes (Matthew 24:45–46).

"Wherefore," the Savior tells us, "be faithful, praying always, having your lamps trimmed and burning, and oil with you, that you may be ready at the coming of the Bridegroom—For behold, verily, verily, I say unto you, that I come quickly" (Doctrine and Covenants 33:17–18).

Jesus Christ lives. I testify that He shall come, as He has promised.

ELDER DALE G. RENLUND

[In March 2020], the Wasatch Front experienced a 5.7-magnitude earthquake. While this is not a significant earthquake and, compared to larger quakes throughout the world, hardly seems worth mentioning, for those of us who had never experienced a moderate-sized earthquake before, this was a disturbing experience.

Prepare for the Savior's Return

As we know, the Salt Lake Temple is currently undergoing a major renovation, including the installation of base isolators that will protect the temple from a potentially larger earthquake. Scientists tell us that there is a 50% chance that the Wasatch Front will experience a 7.2 earthquake in the next 50 years. (Incidentally, 5.7 is bigger than I want to experience ever again!)

To use that as a metaphor for our spiritual lives, I believe there is at least a 50% chance that any of us will experience a spiritual earthquake in our lives in the next 50 years. So I invite you to consider the potential spiritual seismic hits that could come in your life and the spiritual base isolators that you need to have installed to protect you.

Some thoughts I've had include the seismic hit of anxiety for the future. (I am not talking about clinically diagnosed anxiety.) So many things could go wrong in our future, but what can protect us? I would suggest a key base isolator for anxiety is to develop deep faith in Heavenly Father and His plan and unshakable trust in His and Jesus Christ's love.

Other seismic hits could include burdens, challenges, difficulties. Perhaps a seismic hit could be facing perceived unfairness to us individually or to others. Another might be the premature loss of a loved one. There are likely many other life experiences that could end up being a seismic hit to any one of us.

So I invite you to ponder: what are the experiences that could shake your commitment to Heavenly Father and Jesus Christ, and what habits do you need to be working on today to create a base isolator that can absorb the shock of a spiritual seismic hit?

ELDER GERRIT W. GONG

I would like to just offer to our dear members everywhere an apostolic promise that as you also come to listen and hear the voice of the Lord in His scriptures, in His word, that as we read in [Doctrine and Covenants] section 38, ... you'll be prepared and won't need to fear. That in a world that sometimes is tumultuous and full of all kinds of questions and challenges, we can be prepared spiritually if we come to Him; that we can be, it says in verse 39, "the richest of all people." He's not speaking of material riches necessarily. He's saying we can be the richest of all people, for we can have the riches of eternity.

TAKING THE *Sacrament* IS A *Privilege*

ELDER NEIL L. ANDERSEN

Nothing reinforces and sustains our efforts to have repentance as a continuous and constant part of our lives more than our privilege of taking the sacrament each week.

Throughout scripture, the Savior put great emphasis on His disciples partaking of the sacred sacrament.

We can approach the sacrament each week with a broken heart and a contrite spirit.

As disciples of Jesus Christ who strive to "be perfected in him" (Moroni 10:32), we can approach the sacrament each week with a broken heart and a contrite spirit and take upon ourselves the name of Jesus Christ, signifying that we belong to Him.

As we remember Jesus Christ and His suffering, His love for us, and His willingness to take away our sins, we are filled with enormous gratitude and a desire to offer our souls to Him.

PRESIDENT DALLIN H. OAKS

What does the Savior think of me if I continue to make the same or to commit the same sins? (And we're talking about ordinary, day-to-day deviations from what we want to do.) And I would just say, ... the Savior considers you typical of the children of our Heavenly Father. If it weren't typical to make ordinary, day-to-day deviations from the commandments, He wouldn't have told us to partake of the sacrament every Sabbath day. When I was your age, I repeated them all the time. I was jealous of fellows that had more athletic ability than I had, and I had thoughts that I shouldn't entertain. Those are what I call ordinary, day-to-day sins. And that doesn't diminish us in the love and view that our Savior has of us. We're put here on earth to live through that kind of thing and to grow.

ELDER DIETER F. UCHTDORF

[My Wife Harriet and I] visited a place where it is believed the Last Supper occurred. We rested on stone benches

Taking the Sacrament Is a Privilege

under shade trees and read together with friends the sacrament prayers while we considered the significance of this special weekly ordinance.

Although we [were] naturally reminded of the Savior, His ministry, and atoning sacrifice for us while ... in Jerusalem, we can feel an even deeper closeness to our Heavenly Father and His Son through daily seeking His guidance, keeping His commandments, and regularly partaking of the sacrament—regardless of where [we] are in life or geographic location.

God promises us that we may always have His Spirit to be with us. As we ask, seek, and knock, doors will be opened that will lead to His peace and joy.

COMMANDMENTS HELP US *Become* CHRISTLIKE

PRESIDENT HENRY B. EYRING

The gospel is simple. Because of the Savior's atoning sacrifice, we can be cleansed and changed. This begins with faith in Jesus Christ. We believe in Him, trust Him, and depend on Him. That faith leads us to repentance.

We want to show our love for Him by keeping the commandments. Jesus taught by example as He Himself was baptized. Baptism is one of His commandments.

After we are baptized, He promises to give us the gift of the Holy Ghost. We will be guided and comforted, and the Holy Ghost will help us to know the truth. We will feel the Holy Ghost is with us. We will have feelings of peace, love, and joy, and we will have the desire to serve others. We will strive throughout our lives to please the Lord.

As we believe in Him, trust Him, and depend on Him—and do it more frequently—we will feel the comfort of the companionship of the Holy Ghost. We will have the strength to endure any challenge we are presented with and keep the commandments without compulsion.

ELDER GARY E. STEVENSON

When Jesus received the seemingly impossible question, "Which is the great commandment in the law?," He provided a genuine, sacred, divine response: "Thou shalt love the Lord thy God with all thy heart, and with all thy soul, and with all thy mind. This is the first and great commandment. And the second is like unto it, Thou shalt love thy neighbour as thyself" (Matthew 22:36–39).

> *May the Lord's instructions inspire us.*

As we consider each of the two great commandments, let the image of a magnificent suspension bridge with its stately towers soaring toward heaven resonate in your mind's eye. There's this important interdependency between loving the Lord and loving one another. For the Golden Gate Bridge to perform its designed function, both towers are equally strong with equal power to bear the weight of the suspension cables, the roadway, and the traffic crossing the bridge. For any suspension bridge to do what it was built to do, its towers must function together in complete harmony. Likewise, our ability to follow Jesus Christ depends upon our strength and power to live the first and second commandments with balance and equal devotion to both. In the days ahead, when you pass over a majestic suspension bridge, I invite you to remember the two great commandments described by Jesus Christ in the New Testament. May the Lord's instructions inspire us. May our hearts and our minds be lifted upward to love the Lord and turned outward to love our neighbor.

ELDER D. TODD CHRISTOFFERSON

In large letters at the entrance to the temple we see the words, "Holiness to the Lord; The House of the Lord." These powerful words remind us that we should strive to be holy to enter here.

Perfection is not required, but it would be a wonderful thing if we individually worked hard to be at least a little better, a little holier each time we entered the doors of the holy temple.

We can examine our lives from time to time and ask ourselves if there is something unworthy we should put out of our lives, or on the other hand, if there is a Christlike attribute we should more fully cultivate in ourselves.

As we pray and ask God, "What lack I yet?" (Matthew 19:20) let us then act on the impressions that come to us from Him. By what we are becoming day by day, our lives become a more holy offering to the Lord.

PRESIDENT DALLIN H. OAKS

Today, as fewer and fewer individuals understand the great mission of our Lord and Savior, the theme of Jesus Christ needs to dominate our teaching.

Increasing numbers of youth and young adults need to be reclaimed from denying the existence of God or a Savior or from saying that Jesus Christ was only a mortal—a great teacher but not the Son of God with the unique mission outlined in the scriptures and taught by the prophets.

Others believe that while there is probably a God, He makes no commandments that require accountability, so there is no sin.

The most effective method to counteract anti-Christ ideas is teaching and testifying of the reality of Jesus Christ and the necessity of His mission. Our Heavenly Father's plan of salvation is the best answer to many of the questions that are troubling youth and young adults.

The covenants provided in the plan of salvation give us access to His redeeming power. As we seek to know Jesus Christ and come to Him in that covenant relationship, He will give us the power and the guidance to make the right choices, for He is the way, the truth, and the life.

ELDER RONALD A. RASBAND

How true are you? What of your integrity?

Many of you will be asked in the years ahead to bend the rules, to grease wheels, to look the other way, to compromise. Some may even assume that is the way things are done in education, business, government, or your own home. Don't you believe it! Your integrity will be on the line, and the price will never be worth it.

> *Be moral, ethical, and honest. Your word is your bond.*

Be moral, ethical, and honest. Your word is your bond. That is what we learn from making covenants with God. We give the Lord our word, and we hold to it. Remember, another name for Jesus Christ is "the Word."

As we see the standards of the world collapsing in every direction, we are often required to stand strong, defend our faith, and uphold the integrity of the gospel.

Please consider some of the following suggestions that can help you be a little bit better each day.

How true are you? What of your integrity?

Do you desire to stand in holy places?

Do you listen for promptings to help someone else?

When you make a mistake, do you look for someone else to blame? Or can you face the issue and resolve it?

Do you defend others when friends are maligning or being rude to them?

Do you strive to keep the Sabbath day holy? To live the Word of Wisdom?

Do you actively participate in sharing the gospel?

Do you honor and sustain the President of the Church and the Quorum of the Twelve Apostles?

Come to the *House* of the Lord

PRESIDENT RUSSELL M. NELSON

I invite you to come to the temple as often as your circumstances allow.

In the house of the Lord, we focus on Jesus Christ. We learn of Him and His gospel. We make covenants that bind us to Him and to our Heavenly Father. Through these temple experiences and others, we are strengthened to achieve our New Year's resolutions.

ELDER PATRICK KEARON

During the dedication of the Tallahassee Florida Temple . . . , I was again struck by the sacred nature of the house of the Lord.

In this sacred space, where earth and heaven meet, we come to receive solace, peace, and refuge at any time, but especially when we feel lost.

In this sacred space, we can learn more deeply of our eternal identity as cherished daughters and sons of our Heavenly Father, with limitless potential for good and growth.

In this sacred space, our true selves can be found, as we leave the distractions and pettiness of the world outside and receive an extra measure of the Spirit of the Lord to help us hear His still, small voice and meet the demands of life.

> *In this sacred space, our true selves can be found.*

We can be found here in the temple because here in the temple we find Jesus Christ.

ELDER NEIL L. ANDERSEN

The Lord's house is a sacred place between heaven and earth where we better come to know our Father and His Beloved Son, Jesus Christ. . . .

I invite all of us to come to the temple when you are troubled with challenges in your family. Come when decisions confront you. When the world seems burdensome and you seek peace. When you seem defeated and you need added power.

Come when you are happy and all seems well. Come without being asked. Come when you are not in a hurry. Come having forgiven those who have offended you. Come believing.

As we do, the Lord's Spirit will be with us and the beauties of the eternities will be ours.

ELDER GARY E. STEVENSON

If we hope to feel the Spirit of the Lord, we must spend time in places where His Spirit can easily dwell.

Among the most holy of places where we can stand are in the Lord's temples.... I had the distinct pleasure of joining members of The Church of Jesus Christ of Latter-day Saints in Japan as I dedicated the Okinawa Japan Temple.

You may know the country of Japan has a special place in my heart. Visiting always feels like going home. In addition to serving as a missionary for the Church of Jesus Christ as a young man in Japan decades ago, Lesa and I served as mission leaders, and more recently in the Asia North Presidency. In total our family has lived in Japan for seven years.

One of the remarkable aspects of this temple is the fact

that it will serve the Japanese-speaking Okinawa Japan Stake as well as the English-speaking Okinawa Japan Military District.

To consider the history that is part of both of these groups and see them come together to serve the Lord in the temple is simply remarkable.

This temple will allow Okinawan members of the Church of Jesus Christ to honor their ancestors—including the many who faced untimely deaths associated with war.

For those in Okinawa—and for all of us—the temple can bring peace and comfort and unity of heart and mind and respect and devotion to our departed ancestors.

ELDER QUENTIN L. COOK

Everything that we do in temples of The Church of Jesus Christ of Latter-day Saints points to Jesus Christ as the Savior of the world. The Lord organizes eternal families in His temples.

The scriptures are clear that we without our ancestors cannot be made perfect; neither can they without us be made perfect. Their salvation is necessary and essential to our salvation, resulting in the eternal unification of the family (see Doctrine and Covenants 128:15).

This means that the salvation of the whole human family is interdependent and interconnected—like the roots and branches of a great tree. The work performed in the Lord's temples allows us—and our families—to be eternally connected to our loving Heavenly Father.

> *The temple can bring peace and comfort and unity of heart and mind.*

PRESIDENT DALLIN H. OAKS

A temple dedication reminds us to rededicate ourselves to faithfulness in the work of the Lord. A dedicatory prayer offers a temple to the Lord and sets it apart for its eternal purposes in the work of His kingdom. . . .

Because of the restoration of the gospel, we understand our Heavenly Father's plan for His children. The ultimate purpose of the temple is the exaltation of the children of God, which can be attained through the ordinances of the Lord's temples.

Temple teachings center on Jesus Christ. All that is

taught here relates to our Savior. This is His House. This is His work, and the work of His Father. I pray that our Heavenly Father will help us qualify for the blessings that are our destiny as His children.

ELDER RONALD A. RASBAND

Temples, no matter where they are, rise above the ways of the world. Every temple in the world stands as a testament to our faith in eternal life and the joy of spending it with our families and our Heavenly Father. Attending the temple increases our understanding of the Godhead and the everlasting gospel, our commitment to live and teach truth, and our willingness to follow the example of our Lord and Savior, Jesus Christ.

ELDER D. TODD CHRISTOFFERSON

As we enter the temple, we temporarily step out of the world. We lay our problems and challenges down at the door and focus our minds on the things of God, on the ordinances and covenants of salvation and exaltation. We reorient our thoughts and desires to the divine perspective.

We feel more keenly the peace and love emanating from our Heavenly Father and our Savior through the Holy Spirit. We sense that same love for our mothers and fathers of generations past and long to be bound with them eternally. We are renewed in an appreciation of our own infinite worth and in our determination to act accordingly.

As we leave the temple, we find that the problems and challenges we laid down at the entry are still there. We are obliged to shoulder them again. They haven't changed, but gratefully, our time in the temple has changed us. Our perspective is surer and more accurate. We now see that what had seemed overwhelming and impossible can, with the Lord's help, find resolution, and we are more certain of His help.

On the other hand, some small things that had seemed unimportant, we realize need attention now so that they do not become serious matters with detrimental consequences for us or others in time to come. In short, with our time in the temple we have been refined, even if only in a small degree, and heaven is that much closer.

Jesus Christ

IS THE

Strength

OF YOUTH

ELDER NEIL L. ANDERSEN

Sometimes we may wonder how our youth will meet the challenges before them. . . .

Our young people are in the decade of decisions. I have great confidence in them. I pray that they will follow the Savior and gain strength from Him and His sacred Atonement. Jesus Christ is the strength of youth. I pray that they will become more familiar with the quiet promptings of the Holy Ghost. This is a remarkable time to be alive, and our youth will experience unforgettable spiritual moments as they seek the Savior and keep His commandments. The future will be strong as our righteous youth embrace the gospel of Jesus Christ.

> *This is a remarkable time to be alive.*

ELDER GERRIT W. GONG

I pray young people everywhere will feel the love the Savior has for them. As we seek meaningful ways to connect with God and with one another, we will be blessed with spiritual strength in all we do.

PRESIDENT JEFFREY R. HOLLAND

At fourteen or sixteen or seventeen or fifteen or whatever age in your teen years, you're not expected to know everything that President Nelson knows or that your bishop knows or even your parents know. Sometimes you get a little irritated when your parents encourage you one way or the other. Maybe you get irritated with your Young Men and Young Women leaders. . . . But you're not expected to have had the experience they've had. You're not expected to be able to bear the testimony that they bear. You can have the beginning of that testimony—that can come very early. And for many of you, it maybe did come even in your primary years. You can know that the Church is true and that the gospel is true early on. But you get to these teenage years and you're not sure what you do know, and you're maturing, and you want that testimony to grow. Well, look, just be reassured that that happens to everybody. I went through that, Sister Holland went through that, everybody I know, one way or the other, goes through that because it's a matter of our maturation in the gospel. And I want you to hang on. I want you to persevere in that quest, because it'll matter all the days of your life that you stay in there, that you keep fighting the fight.

ELDER DIETER F. UCHTDORF

Moral agency is one of life's greatest gifts from our loving Heavenly Father. The *For the Strength of Youth* guide gives our rising generation guidance on how to use their moral agency and how to make wise choices as they seek to follow Jesus Christ.

Often parents and leaders direct their youth to the *FSY* guide to help them with their choices, and I am extremely grateful for this effort. I also want to remind each of us that it is vital for parents, adults, and leaders to read the guide and speak with our rising generation about the content.

Whenever I read the *FSY* guide, I am lifted up spiritually

and strengthened by the inspired principles and counsel included. How I wish I had something like this when I was growing up. Now I am grateful to be blessed by it as an adult, a grandfather, and great-grandfather.

For the Strength of Youth teaches eternal truths about the Savior and His way. It helps us to make the right choices based on divine truths. It shares promised blessings that Heavenly Father extends to all who desire to follow Him. I invite you to read, ponder, apply, and share this precious guide!

> *Moral agency is one of life's greatest gifts.*

ELDER DAVID A. BEDNAR

We teach our youth ... that all people are your brothers and sisters, including, of course, people who are different from you or disagree with you. To assist our young people in the ongoing process of learning correct principles for themselves, we invite them to be agents who act on what they are learning, and not just objects who are acted upon. One of the best ways to promote such action is by trusting and guiding young people to lead. Service, ultimately, is where learning and acting come together, helping our youth to focus on serving and blessing other people instead of just on themselves. Through service, youth can become more tolerant, learn to respect and even love people different from themselves, and become strong representatives for countries and cultures significantly different from their own. Through learning, acting, and serving, the youth of The Church of Jesus Christ of Latter-day Saints are growing step-by-step toward becoming, according to our faith, true disciples of Jesus Christ.

FEEL THE *Joy* OF *Christmas*

ELDER ULISSES SOARES

Living in a world with increasing darkness, Jesus Christ is the true light that strengthens our life. In the scriptures, the word light is always connected to Jesus Christ. Beginning with His birth, a star lit the way for the Wise Men to find the infant in the manger. Likewise, "great lights in heaven"—along with the sky never darkening for "two days and a night" in the New World—signified the birth of Jesus Christ (Helaman 14:3–4). He is referred to as "the true Light, which lighteth every man that cometh into the world" (John 1:9), "an everlasting light" (Isaiah 60:19), and the "light of the world" (John 8:12). When God the Father and His Son, Jesus Christ, appeared to Joseph Smith as a "pillar of light," their "brightness and glory [defied] all description" (Joseph Smith–History 1:16–17). As we seek Jesus Christ and embrace His light, we become His children—"children of light" (John 12:36). At Christmas and always, may we follow Him, walking in the light of His love.

DIRECT MESSAGES

ELDER PATRICK KEARON

I love the time of year when we gather as families and loved ones to remember the birth of our Savior. Yet, amid our gatherings, gifts, and events, our schedules can become overwhelming, and we may feel weighed down by the pressures of the holiday. Sometimes the expectations we impose upon ourselves overshadow the joy of the season rather than magnifying it.

Let us not become so busy and weary that we miss the true focus of Christmas—worshipping the newborn King and offering Him our own personal gift.

ELDER GARY E. STEVENSON

At Christmastime we often sing the song "Joy to the World." A wonderful verse in this song always stands out to me:

"Let every heart prepare him room."

Amongst all the events of the season, Christmas seems like an ideal time for us to thoughtfully evaluate the status of our hearts.

You might ask yourself, "Is my heart prepared to receive the Savior?" How can you prepare room in your heart for Christ—especially during this busy yet wonderful season?

In order for us to receive Him in our hearts, surely they must be humble like His. I promise that by making room in our hearts for the Savior, this wonderful time of year will be made more joyous. You will feel even greater the magnificence of His birth, life, and light to all the world.

PRESIDENT DALLIN H. OAKS

What is the meaning of the phrase "peace on earth, good will toward men" (see Luke 2:14), shared often during the Christmas season?

The heavenly hosts proclaimed good will to all men—to casual friends and to strangers.

The Savior taught, "Love thy neighbour as thyself" (Matthew 22:39). He even taught that we should love our enemies, bless them that curse us, do good to them that hate us, and pray for them who despitefully use us and persecute us.

As we work toward the goal expressed in those teachings, Christmas should be a time for forgiving, a time to heal old wounds and restore relationships that have gone awry. Christmas is a time to extend ourselves beyond our normal ties of love and friendship.

PRESIDENT RUSSELL M. NELSON

[During the] Christmas season, will you let your light shine? Amid all the hustle and bustle of gifts and gatherings, will you let your life reflect the life and love of Jesus Christ? With the dawning of each day, could you identify someone who needs your light? Reach out to that person by phone, video chat, or send a text or a note. Perform a quiet act of service to help someone nearby. Bring a new friend into your circle. Help someone turn to the Savior and find enduring peace and divine rest.

> *The world needs the light of Jesus Christ. And the world needs your light.*

There is no better way to celebrate the birth of Jesus Christ than by lifting, loving, and serving others. The world needs the light of Jesus Christ. And the world needs your light. God be thanked for loving us enough to send His Only Begotten Son. Jesus Christ changed the world for each of us with His atoning sacrifice. He is the light of the world. He is the light we need to hold up. He is the light that fills us with goodwill toward all people. I love the Lord Jesus Christ and testify that He lives. As we celebrate His birth in Bethlehem, let us emulate His life of lovingkindness. May you and your loved ones be filled with His light and joy for now and always.

ELDER GERRIT W. GONG

For many of us, Christmas is a joyful season. At the same time, some of us can feel alone, lost, isolated, or sad.

Let us celebrate Christmas this year by following Jesus Christ to do all we can to make sure there is room in His inn for each of us.

As we do so, we will find the true meaning of Christmas.

ELDER DALE G. RENLUND

As President Russell M. Nelson taught, "One of the best ways we can honor the Savior is to become a peacemaker" ("Peacemakers Needed," *Liahona*, May 2023).

I am reminded of a wonderful Christmas tradition that

blended an ancient African custom with Christian teachings. This tradition developed in some villages in West and Central Africa. With ongoing urbanization, the custom is rapidly diminishing.

A man from one of these villages told me that in his small village there was a Christmas tradition wherein everyone with a dispute with another villager met on the morning of Christmas Eve with the village chief. The chief would listen and seek to resolve the dispute to the satisfaction of both parties.

This process of dispute resolution would go on all day, but at the end of the day, no villager had an unresolved dispute with another villager. The purpose of the tradition was to enable the villagers to be ready the next day to celebrate the birth of the Prince of Peace. Each needed to let go of contention to properly bring in the Christmas Day.

Perhaps one way we can honor the Savior this Christmas is by letting go of grudges, seeking forgiveness, and granting forgiveness. We can let the pure love of Christ be the antidote to contention. As we do so, we will be ready to bring in the Prince of Peace on Christmas Day.

Feel the Joy of Christmas

PRESIDENT JEFFREY R. HOLLAND

Unless we see all the meaning and joy of Christmas—the whole of Christ's life, His profound mission, the end as well as the beginning—then Christmas will be just another day off work with food and fun and festivities.

The true meaning—the unique, joyous meaning—of the birth of Jesus Christ was not confined to those first hours in Bethlehem but would be realized in the life He would lead and in His death, in His triumphant atoning sacrifice, and in His prison-bursting Resurrection. These are the realities that make Christmas joyful.

This year, let us remember the greatest gift ever given: the Atonement and Resurrection of the Lord Jesus Christ.

> *Let us celebrate Christmas this year by following Jesus Christ.*

Prophets and Apostles *Testify* of Christ and Speak *Truth*

PRESIDENT JEFFREY R. HOLLAND

My testimony to the Church and to the world is that this is true. This is God's very truth. This is not a fairy tale. This is not something that I get up every morning and ask myself, "How can I go fool another group of people today? How can I go pretend that something's true? How can I go work a great fiction on the public?"

I would not do that. And my life is worth more to me than that, and my witness to my children and my children's children is worth more than that—means more than that. My integrity is more than that. I get up every morning saying not, "How can I pretend? How can I act like this is true?" My plea every morning of my life is, "How can I convey what I know to be more true than anything on the face of this earth? How can I convey to some person, or persons, the reality of the divinity of the Lord Jesus Christ, the fact that God lives, that the heavens are open?" I have a commission to stand by the Savior of the world, to defend

Him, and defend the rock that He is. Joseph Smith and Hyrum did not sit in Carthage Jail ready to be executed by a mob, they did not pull out the Book of Mormon and say, "Let's tell some jokes from this book we made up." No one would do that. No one would do that. They read from that book because they knew it was true and they knew it would be their salvation. A missionary once asked me, "Elder Holland, would you give your life for the Church?" And I said, "Elder, I *am* giving my life for the Church. Every day I'm giving my life for the Church because I know it's true."

PRESIDENT HENRY B. EYRING

A testimony of the Resurrection of Jesus Christ is a source of both hope and determination. He lives, and because of His sacrifice, we will be resurrected and sanctified. Jesus is the risen Christ, our Savior, and our perfect example and guide to eternal life. I pray that we may, with all our hearts for all our lives, remember His sacrifice and His love of us.

> *Jesus is the risen Christ, our Savior, and our perfect example.*

ELDER ULISSES SOARES

I have always loved the Primary song that says, "I know my Father lives and loves me too. The Spirit whispers this to me and tells me it is true, and tells me it is true" (*Children's Songbook*, 5). In this spirit, I would like to share my testimony with you.... My testimony was built line upon line and continues to grow as I continuously search with a sincere heart to more fully understand the word of God.

I know Jesus is the Christ. I know He lives. I know He suffered for my sins and was resurrected and gave me a chance to change my behavior. I know He forgot Himself for me; He turned away from His own desires and did exactly what the Father asked Him to do. Even in that very moment of great suffering, He denied Himself and did what the Father would have Him do.

I know our Heavenly Father lives and listens to our prayers. I testify to you that He understands pain. I know this is the true Church of Jesus Christ on earth. The Lord truly commenced the Restoration of His gospel and His priesthood through the Prophet Joseph Smith. I love my Savior and my Heavenly Father, and I love to serve Them.

PRESIDENT JEFFREY R. HOLLAND

I was studying in the Pearl of Great Price, [and I] came across another verse that . . . had a tremendous impact on me. This is from Moses 7: "And it came to pass that the Lord spake unto Enoch, and told Enoch all the doings of the children of men; wherefore Enoch knew, and looked upon their wickedness, and their misery," those two go together, "and wept and stretched forth his arms, and his heart swelled wide as eternity; and his bowels yearned; and all eternity shook" [v. 41].

I don't know why that verse had such an impact on me. I've read it before, but the idea of a prophet conversing with God and sensing the mission and opening his arms and opening his heart and all eternity shakes. Maybe I feel stronger about that in my role than an average Latter-day Saint would, but I'm going to try to weep for people's misery and open my arms to all eternity and see if I can make eternity shake. I think that's what an Apostle, or a prophet, is supposed to do.

Prophets and Apostles Testify of Christ and Speak Truth

PRESIDENT HENRY B. EYRING

In a message posted to social media channels 100 days before his September 9th birthday, President Nelson invited us in this way: "One spiritual offering that would brighten my life is for each of us to reach out to the one in our lives who may be feeling lost or alone. Over the coming months, I invite you to consider prayerfully, who do you know who may be discouraged?"

As many of you did, I accepted the prophet's invitation to pray. It was confirmed for me what I had learned when I was a little boy, that Heavenly Father hears prayers we offer in faith and in the name of Jesus Christ. As a child, it was to find something I had lost. When I found them, I felt Their love.

When I prayed in answer to President Russell M. Nelson's invitation, names and faces of friends came into my mind. I knew little of the personal challenges they faced. I prayed for them before I called. One said they had already felt my prayers for them. Another said that it had been an especially hard day. From those experiences, I had at least three truths reconfirmed for me by accepting the invitation from the living prophet of God. First, Heavenly

Father hears and answers our prayers promptly when we ask Him how we can help one of His children. Second, the Lord goes before us with His message of love for them. And third, the prophet of God is the Lord's true servant and leads us with loving invitations. I am grateful for the blessing of having heard and accepted his one hundredth birthday invitation. It was a gift of love that will last in my heart forever.

ELDER DALE G. RENLUND

I am grateful for the responsibility to be a special witness of Jesus Christ in all the world. It is a joy to witness of His living reality, His majesty and power, and His great compassion for all of Heavenly Father's children.

PRESIDENT JEFFREY R. HOLLAND

For three decades, it has been my honor and privilege to associate with the members of the Quorum of the Twelve Apostles of The Church of Jesus Christ of Latter-day Saints. Without exception, every one of these men has helped me become a better disciple of Jesus Christ.

Prophets and Apostles Testify of Christ and Speak Truth

As we gathered recently to take a quorum photo, I felt a sense of immense gratitude to be part of an ongoing order of ancient and modern-day disciples of Jesus Christ.

The names and faces of those in this quorum change over time, but that which is essential remains: each apostle has accepted the charge "to be a special witness of the name of Christ in all the world." No sweeter work could ever be given to anyone, nor any finer group of men with which to do it.

> *Our Heavenly Father and His Beloved Son love us, are aware of us, and will bless each of us.*

PRESIDENT RUSSELL M. NELSON

We rejoice in the peace that radiates from the Lord Jesus Christ. It will continue to fill us with hope and joy. Our Heavenly Father and His Beloved Son love us, are aware of us, and will bless each of us. I love you, dear brothers and sisters, and assure you that wonderful days are ahead. Our commitment to follow the Lord is everlasting.